BLOSSOM

Cultivating More Joy and Success in Life and Business

Nancy Rae Lohman

Dedication

To Lowell Lohman with all my love.
Lowell encouraged me to write this book.
His vision and belief in me have made me
Cinderella – at least *his* Cinderella –
and that is all that matters to me.

Contents

Part II: Give Well

Chapter 4: Appreciate * 85

Express Gratitude
The Impact of the Thank You Note
Fill a Gratitude Box
Practice Random Acts of Kindness
Be Generous

Chapter 5: Befriend * 100

Nurture Friendships
Support Your Friends' Victories
Enjoy the Holidays
Create Ceremonies and Celebrations
Give Meaningful Gifts
Be the Keeper of Memories
Develop a Happiness Lifestyle

Part III: Live Well

Chapter 6: Prepare Yourself * 129

Move Forward by Letting Go of the Past
Believe You Can Do It and You Can!
Prepare: Make a Plan and Work Your Plan
Be Open to Opportunity and Be Optimistic
Invest in Your Personal and Professional
    Growth
It's Jack Nicklaus Time!
Break the People-Pleasing Habit
Follow Up and Follow Through
Be Resilient

Preface

"Next to God we are indebted to women,
first for life itself,
and then for making it worth living."
Dr. Mary McLeod Bethune

The ideas in this book stem from years of requests by local and professional organizations asking my husband and me to speak on leadership and success. I wanted to memorialize in writing the ideas that helped me navigate business and life and enabled me to enjoy a contentment that may be rare.

These are leadership and life experiences that I have lived through, at times vicariously, which have directly or unexpectedly provided clarity. I have also benefited from the advice of excellent books and publications. In life and work I have at times tried and succeeded and I have sometimes tried and failed. I have learned valuable lessons that have inspired me to pursue, live and cherish a fulfilled life. These lessons gave me direction and helped me process my thoughts and develop my own internal guiding light. I will be forever grateful for the wisdom I have gathered from the amazing individuals and writers who have been a part of my life's journey. I am excited to share these insights with you in the hope of supporting women and their ambitions.

*****

Several years ago, our family sold our funeral homes and cemeteries after serving our community for nearly two decades. Through my experience in the death-care industry as a business owner, licensed funeral director and certified celebrant, I realize a person's true resume is their eulogy. Our legacy is what lives on in others. Poignant eulogies include stories describing how people's lives were forever shaped and inspired by the person who had died. Those were "aha" moments for me time and time again, as I sat in the back of funeral home chapels, churches and synagogues. Moments when I gained valuable insights about leading, giving and living well. So much of what I have learned has come from people I never met or met only briefly. I was inspired, through stories shared by their family, friends, colleagues and pastors, to reflect on my own life and make changes based on their account of a life well-lived.

Through my corporate life, our family business and from eulogies, I realize a woman's life in business can be described as yin and yang. We are expected to be tender and tough. We are nurtured to be nice, loving, sympathetic and caring and yet we also find ourselves in situations that require us to be strong. Yin and yang.

Funeral directing was an immensely gratifying occupation most of the time. It is a profession I never contemplated for myself. In fact, when my husband, Lowell, asked me to become a funeral director he said, "I'll build it if you run it." And I said, "I can't be a funeral director, I wear fuchsia!" It is a profession wrought with dichotomies. There is that yin and yang again. On the one hand, compassion and empathy were needed with each family we served. On the other hand, the financial risks of the business and the challenging liabilities of business ownership were demanding and intense. Add to that the rise in the popularity of cremation, which continues to diminish financial returns. At times I was embraced as a welcome member of a family during a fragile and tender moment in their lives and at other times I was a witness to, even a target of, anger, hostility and resentment.

Overall and in the end, I know that we grieve because we love, and I know I am a better person for having served in the profession. I know that mourning is the outward way in which we grieve together a life lost because we are establishing the significance of the person who has died. It provides a moment to connect with others and share our grief. Funeral rituals and celebrations of life are the mourning traditions that provide the steps we need to slowly but surely move forward and heal.

A good deal of my career is behind me and I have purposely slowed my hamster wheel. My greater self-assurance and slower pace have allowed me to be more reflective. I am lucky to have had a loving mother who was also a solid role model and mentor. It was her influence that led to my perspective that gender makes no difference when it comes to achieving your goals. Anything is attainable if you work hard enough and smart enough. I attribute my work ethic, independence, self-reliance, resourcefulness and belief in the value of education to her. I have also been lucky to have a loving and supportive husband who is a charismatic leader and visionary. His influence has been tremendous in my life; he is supportive of me and all women in leadership roles. I am assertive and can be vocal; I may come across as tough at times. However, I have often found myself seeking the approval of others to the detriment of my own well-being. Although I enjoy being a woman with all the accoutrements of femininity (heels, dresses, makeup and jewelry), I have never once felt I was limited in any way because of my gender. In fact, I have always felt strongly that I was only limited if I allowed myself to be.

Introduction

"Success can make you go one of two ways.
It can make you a prima donna,
or it can smooth the edges, take away the insecurities
and let the nice things come out."
Barbara Walters

This book provides navigational tools – nuggets in the form of life lessons and business lessons. In our professional and personal lives, we move through our challenges and beyond them by focusing on leading ourselves well, giving well and living well.

Most of us are trying to live fulfilling lives, successfully balancing a variety of roles. It is not easy at times. We worry about current commitments and past mistakes. We contemplate how decisions will affect us and the others we care about. We wonder how we can truly make a difference and how our legacy will be defined.

I once shared with a woman who had been diagnosed with cancer: "We'll ride the waves with you till the storm calms." I know she was surrounded with love, compassion and care. But I wanted her to know I was among those supporting her. Isn't that what we all need, even if we are not facing a serious health crisis as she was? From time to time, we all find our life challenges nearly insurmountable, which is why we must draw on those mantras that bear repeating when we need them most. It is why we need others. We need authentic, loyal, loving friends and family to ride the waves with us – unconditionally.

For many women, our lives can often be described as yin and yang. I know mine is. In Chinese philosophy yin and yang means the dark opposed to the bright. It describes the complementary and connected forces of opposites. The yin and yang manifest in our lives as we achieve outstanding success yet struggle with difficult challenges, sometimes simultaneously. We are both warm and giving yet systematic, task oriented, assertive and highly organized. Yin and yang.

Successful people take responsibility for failures but process negative feelings and thoughts, then let them go. We choose to forgive ourselves. We learn from our mistakes, but do not allow them to imprison us. We place a high value on the right to find our own brand of happiness and inner peace. We reflect on our attitude and our outlook. We practice empowering habits in all areas of life. We blossom. Yet we all need a little encouragement now and then. Our personal and professional success in life is a result of making proper choices, choosing positive influences and finding a healthy balance.

BLOSSOM

Cultivating More Joy and Success
in Life and Business

Part I

Lead Well

Chapter 1

Lead Yourself to Better Lead Others

"In the future, there will be no female leaders.
There will just be leaders."
Sheryl Sandberg

Go the Extra Mile

"I never dreamed about success. I worked for it."
Estee Lauder

The most successful people are those who stay focused on their mission. They take charge and most importantly they do what is right. They keep their eyes on the big picture and know what they ultimately want to accomplish. They plan, exercise self-discipline and do not allow small setbacks to distract them. Organizational leadership and professional success are not about prestige or power. Successful individuals take responsibility for an organization's well-being and growth, as well as their own.

The largest cemetery serving our community, Bellevue-Cedar Hill, was in big trouble. Frequent headlines and stories in the news media detailed the problems: botched burials, misplaced and lost bodies, missing baby caskets, allegations that gold teeth were stolen from bodies, unkempt and overgrown grounds, decaying tombstones, and other problems left the families of the deceased angry and demanding answers.

Our son Ty and I encouraged my husband Lowell to purchase the properties. We told Lowell that our family, including Lowell's brother Victor Lohman, could provide the personnel and the expertise to turn the business around and to resolve the situations plaguing the various locations. We knew there would be scrutiny in the public spotlight while we worked to right the wrongs. We knew we would have to spend hundreds of thousands of dollars to rehabilitate and renovate the property and even more to turn it into a first-class organization. We knew it would take tremendous effort by all four of us. We knew we could do it. In truth, it was the most rewarding experience of our lives.

Success requires meaningful work and the perseverance driven by a passionate desire to achieve goals. Restoring Daytona Memorial Park and Funeral Home* was meaningful work. It was hard work and we were passionate about it. It involved difficult decisions and even more difficult conversations with families. A successful person knows and understands their mission. They set clear goals – specific and measurable goals. They articulate and communicate goals and expectations to others. They know exactly what they want to achieve, where they want to go, what must occur. They are passionate. Then they create a plan that keeps them individually and as a team motivated to get there. (*The Lohmans changed the name of the cemetery and funeral home as part of their rebranding effort.)

Know Your Strengths and Weaknesses

"To be somebody, a woman does not need to be more like a man, she has to be more of a woman."
Sally E. Shaywitz

We are more likely to flourish when we are given the opportunity to act on our strengths and do what we do best, according to author Barbara Fredrickson. Exercising our strengths can be profoundly gratifying, which is why learning about our strengths and focusing on ways to use them can be energizing. Some strengths define the types of contributions we are most poised to provide. So reshaping your work life and personal life to maximize your strengths promises to provide greater fulfillment in your life.

We all have strengths *and* weaknesses. Learning how to perform successfully in life by utilizing our strengths and relying on teammates to compensate for our weaknesses can help us be more successful. First, though, we must identify them. The road to wisdom requires knowledge of ourselves. "The unexamined life is not worth living," said Socrates in *Plato's Apology*, "success and power have often crowded out of a leader's life a willingness to become accountable to others."

As our family developed our funeral home and cemetery business, the role of each family member became clearer. As we grew, I recognized how much I did not enjoy the daily routine of managing. It was not one of my strengths. I have to admit I feel guilty as I write these words. Don't we need to love managing if we are in business? Don't we need to excel at it to be successful? I wanted to create unique ways to celebrate lives. I enjoyed orchestrating flawless funeral services. I wanted every family to be overwhelmed with gratitude once they were served by the Lohman family and staff. I wanted to teach and empower our staff to find ways to wow families. But I did not want to manage the daily, routine behind-the-scenes tasks and functions.

The solution was to hire a Senior Funeral Director. Someone who would support our vision to provide outstanding service deliverables for every family. And someone whose forte was managing daily schedules, routines, and personnel issues. I re-

alized that to be an effective leader you need to surround yourself with people who possess the skills
that you do not. Delegate to them the tasks or responsibilities that allow them to use their strengths.

As I previously revealed, there were four
Lohmans in our family business: my husband Lowell, our son Ty, my brother-in-law Victor, and myself. One day I requested that each Lohman read
StrengthsFinder 2.0 by Tom Rath and take the online
test at the end of the book. The test identifies which
five key strengths are innate within you and provides advice on how to use those strengths in your
work and personal life. For me, even more importantly, it offered suggestions on how to work with
and relate to others based on their strengths. It was
a valuable tool in self-awareness for me, one that
led to my understanding of why I needed a Senior
Funeral Director. Rath argues that we should forget about fixing our weaknesses and instead, go all
in on our strengths. Our weaknesses will always be
weaknesses no matter how much we work on them.
Instead, focus on enhancing strengths.

Once I began a more intentional process
of understanding my strengths and weaknesses,
I learned to embrace them. I acknowledged my
weaknesses, then identified ways I could utilize
and improve my strengths. What followed was
more congruency in my life. Aligning work and
other activities with our innate strengths brings

more contentment and satisfaction. Some of us may not necessarily find all our fulfillment in our day jobs. Bills must be paid, and we must financially support ourselves. So perhaps the answer lies in an extracurricular activity; that is what I found. Self-awareness can help us find specific ways to align our strengths with our life choices.

Maintain Your Integrity
"Truth is the only safe ground to stand upon."
Elizabeth Cady Stanton

Integrity is "the state of being complete, uni-fied." When you have integrity, your words and actions match. You are who you are, no matter where you are or who you are with, even if you are alone. Integrity helps create consistency and helps you make proper choices. Do you make decisions that are best for your company/organization – or best for you? Integrity helps you share the accolades. Do you give credit when others have helped you?

When I was 10, I joined my classmates on a field trip to the Center of Science and Industry in Columbus, Ohio. The experience ended with a walk through the gift shop on our way out of the building. I wanted a souvenir, a small round white button that said COSI in big bold black letters. It was only ten cents, but I had no money. So, I took it. I stole a ten-cent button. For days after our field trip,

I felt terrible about what I had done. Afraid to admit to my parents what had happened, I kept the button in a little jewelry box, vowing to return it. I pictured my next visit to the museum, where I would sneak the button back onto the rack in the gift shop. But the opportunity never came. I harbored my guilt, vowing never to steal again, knowing even at that young age that I had secretly failed myself and my family. I had not lived up to my own moral standards or my family's expectations of who I was. Somewhere along the line I lost the button but never forgot the lesson it taught me and the commitment to honesty I made in my life moving forward. When I reached the age where I finally had discretionary income – that point when I was no longer upside down financially – I sent the museum and science center a significant and anonymous donation. It did not rectify what I did, but the restitution helped me own the mistake I made and reinforced the lesson I had learned.

Ask yourself these questions: Am I the same person when no one is looking as I am when all eyes are upon me? John Hawkins, author of the book *Leadership as a Lifestyle*, reminds us, "It is important that we expect leaders to be role models and to lead us in producing significant results. The standards and values that they live by set the bar for the others in the organization."

USAF Reserve Major General William Cohen held the position of professor of leadership at California State University. He taught eight laws of leadership, which began with the tenet that a leader must maintain absolute integrity: "You cannot maintain your integrity 90 percent and be a leader. It's got to be 100 percent."

At the funeral home, there were times when we would finish meeting with a family to plan their loved one's services or we would conduct a funeral service, and then we would return to our back offices. "You just can't make this stuff up," we said on more than one occasion. One day I was meeting with a brother and sister who had just lost their father. Their mother was still alive but unable, physically or emotionally, to meet with me. As we discussed various choices for their father's services, the brother and sister often questioned each other and themselves, always wondering if they were doing what their mother would want. They were worried that their own self-interests might conflict with the right thing to do in their mother's eyes. I thought they were a lovely example of concerned siblings grieving their father's death and caring for their mother's feelings. When they were leaving the funeral home, the brother turned to me and said, "Nancy, you must think we're crazy!" To which I replied, "I've seen crazy and you aren't even close!"

Far too often I saw a lack of integrity. I was frequently reminded that maintaining integrity is challenging, especially in the midst of crisis. A crisis can test integrity in a way that everyday life may not. When a crisis comes, integrity or a lack of integrity will play out. The damage happens in real time, motivated by a variety of influences, including power and greed. It made for interesting, even wildly unimaginable dynamics at the funeral home.

In John Maxwell's book *Developing the Leader Within You,* he declares five oaths of integrity: "I will live what I teach, I will do what I say, I will be honest with others, I will put what is best for others ahead of what is best for me, and I will be transparent and vulnerable." Always maintain your integrity. It will likely be tested.

Make Proper Choices

"Don't compromise yourself.
You are all you've got!"
Janis Joplin

Making a choice is a thought process. Proper choices are intentional decisions based on (a sometimes quick) analysis. Confidence emerges when you own your decisions even if that means admitting you should have made some decisions differently. But experience allows you to continue making more and more *proper* decisions that create less drama – with decisions that provide better outcomes, not worse. Being decisive doesn't mean being rash.

It means you are making decisions with your core values firmly in place.

As I mentioned earlier, there have been dozens of "aha" moments in my life while sitting alone in the last pew at the back of a church as a funeral director. I have listened to poignant stories of the ways in which people lived that left indelible marks on the lives of their family and friends. These life lessons were and are their legacies.

It was a Saturday afternoon and the church was packed. There was not a single open seat and I am certain the church sat at least five hundred. The woman who had died was amazing: she was beautiful, vivacious and accomplished. Her husband spoke of her kindness and beauty, how she loved life and loved most everything and everyone in it. He spoke of the breadth of her accomplishments, her advanced degrees, her athletic achievements and her zest for life. Then he told us how she had done so much and so well. He said she had two rules: always be nice to everyone regardless of their position in life and remember that life is all about making proper choices.

He talked about how devoted she was to daily exercise and how she was a careful and disciplined eater. Most of us know those are clearly proper choices. He also shared that her choices in life were made based on how they would affect her and the two of them in the short term and the long term. She made decisions based on how they would affect everyone she loved, cared for and worked with. He said she made a choice to love everyone with a whole heart and made a choice to always remain humble. At the end of his eulogy he said, "Jesus gave us only two rules: Love God and love thy neighbor as thyself. She did the second better than anyone else I know."

Making proper choices gives you the power to impact your life. Once you are clear on your values and standards, your choices become clearer. Proper choices lessen regret – and regret can be difficult. I regretted not making the proper choice in that science center gift shop. But regret isn't always negative. It might mean you learned the hard way. Learning from a poor decision is important. I learned I would never again take anything that did not rightfully belong to me. Processing a poor decision is important. Then, making amends for a poor outcome is critical. It did not make it right, but I felt better recognizing and admitting my poor decision, sending an apology letter and making a generous donation to the science center. Revisiting moments and decisions you regret can lead to paralysis through fear of making the same mistake again. If your future decisions are based firmly on your values, then once you make a choice, embrace it. Know that it is the proper choice after evaluating all the available information and weighing the outcomes and consequences with your own standards clearly in mind. This lessens the likelihood of the "what if only" thoughts that decrease your satisfaction with your decision. Ultimately this second-guessing diminishes the joy of the choice you made. Proper choices and good decision-making lead to happiness, joy, fulfillment and purpose.

Develop Trust

"People follow leaders by choice.
Without trust, at best you get compliance."
Jesse Lyn Stoner

A team's strength depends on the connection each person has with another – which ultimately comes down to trust. Trust is a belief in the reliability of each team member. Highly reputable and admired organizations have a company culture with a high degree of mutual respect and trustworthiness among and across the board of directors, management team and associates. Joseph Michelli, author of *The New Gold Standard*, shared, "While human failings occur within Ritz-Carlton leadership, the standard has been set to foster trust, and it is producing results that trickle down to the day-to-day experiences of frontline workers. Clearly, Ritz-Carlton leadership understands the importance of creating an environment of respect at all touchpoints in the employee's journey. It is even a better testament to the impact of trust when guests recognize the confidence that frontline workers have in their leadership."

A great team requires great relationships. It is important to remember that people do not experience your intentions, they experience your behaviors. Your behaviors are either admired or disappointing to others. Trust is earned through your behavior, not granted by your position.

After we had purchased the troubled cemetery and funeral home locations from receivership, a story broke in our local newspaper about our new endeavor. A gentleman called the cemetery the day after he read the article in the paper. He was interested in an above-ground private estate. On the day he came to the cemetery to meet with Lowell, he mentioned the article to me. I remember him saying, "I called because of that last line of the article and what you said, Nancy." I turned to the article to read what had been quoted in the final sentences of the article: Asked why they are repairing the rear of the mausoleum where visitors aren't allowed to go, Nancy Lohman said, "Because we know it's there." We were earning his trust by our behavior.

"Trust is belief in the reliability of a person," writes Urban Meyer, retired college football coach, in his book *Above the Line: Lessons in Leadership and Life from a Championship Season*. "The strength of a team is determined by the strength of the connection – their trust within the team. A great team requires great relationships. Individuals with credibility are fully believable because they are fully trusted." Warren Bennis and Burt Nanus (as quoted by author John Maxwell) call trust "the glue that binds followers and leaders together." Trust requires time. Trust requires transparency. Trust requires consistency. Trust requires demonstration.

Know Your Values and Know They Impact Everything

"Lasting change is a series of compromises.
And compromise is all right,
as long as your values don't change."
Jane Goodall

Whether it is your family, your business or an organization you belong to, your core values impact others around you and ultimately your long-term success. Core values may include honesty, integrity, loyalty and a strong work ethic. A list is generally easy to come up with and a good exercise. What are the specific values at *your* "core" – the cornerstone of all your actions? What is deep in your heart, always in the back of your mind and reflected in every decision and action you take? How do you live up to your core values daily?

Honesty or truthfulness is often at the top of

everyone's list. And it deserves that place. Benjamin Franklin's immortal adage, "Honesty is the best policy," has been passed down from one generation to another for more than a century. As children most of us were told the story of George Washington and the cherry tree, the most well-known legend about him. The original story states that when Washington was six years old, he received a hatchet as a gift and damaged his father's cherry tree. When his father discovered what had happened, he became angry and confronted young George, who bravely admitted, "I cannot tell a lie ... I did cut it with my hatchet." Washington's father embraced him and rejoiced that his son's honesty was worth more than a thousand trees.

Honesty is not that easy. Often, we rationalize our lack of honesty as a fib, a white lie, a way we protect someone from a truth that may hurt their feelings. But deception can be stressful. In *Mark Twain's Notebook*, the master exaggerator confesses, "If you tell the truth, you don't have to remember anything."

I was often reminded of the importance of honesty during my funeral home career. Delicate situations required both honesty and gentleness. Honesty was required not only from us, but often from the family or friend who became our point of contact for funeral arrangements. One Saturday I met with two close friends of an older person who had died. Apparently, the deceased had no surviving relatives. I thought the arrangements went well, the two friends seemed satisfied with the services we had planned together and I believed they left feeling comfortable with all the details. An hour passed and I received a sobering call from the couple asking if they could come in again and meet with me. Their tone was grave. My mind raced with what could have gone wrong. I worked back through our arrangement conference in my mind. I thought our meeting had flowed nicely. When they came into the funeral home, they explained to me that they had been contacted by estranged family members who now wanted to attend the service. I could not imagine why that would be so troubling. Then they explained that the person who had died was a woman, but his relatives knew him only while he was a man. They asked me to keep this information from the family and have a simple graveside service. Can you imagine the stress of having to use a singular pronoun with an unspecified antecedent throughout the funeral service, saying "they" instead of "he" or "she"? Phew! Of course, the friends who had planned the service thought they had been successful with their hidden truth until after the service concluded, when conversations began between family and friends. I could not hear the conversations, but I did not need to – the nonverbal expressions on their faces said it all.

"Oh! What a tangled web we weave, when first we practice to deceive," was written more than 200 years ago. Sir Walter Scott, best-selling author of novels, plays and poems, coined that famous quote in 1808, although it is often attributed to William Shakespeare. It is a powerful and enduring idiom about the value of honesty. When you lie or act dishonestly, as Mark Twain points out, you are initiating a story that you must remember, and usually you initiate other problems as well. The story, the lie, the problem often has a domino effect – and the complications can grow until eventually they are out of control.

Chapter 2

Inspire & Encourage

"Make the most of yourself (and others)
by fanning the tiny,
inner sparks of possibility into
flames of achievement."
Golda Meir

Be a Cheerleader

"Amazing things happen when
women help other women."
Kasia Gospos

Be "up," positive, full of energy and cheer people on. Your motivation needs to be visible and authentic. If you are not excited and inspired, how can you expect those around you to be enthusiastic? As a leader your mindset matters and can be felt throughout your organization. Staying focused on positives such as finding solutions will have a tremendous impact on others.

Jack Welch of General Electric, ranked one of

the best CEOs of the 20th century, agreed that critical keys to leadership are required for an organization to be successful. "In order to get your employees engaged, you need to be rich with your praise, cheer them on, love to watch them grow and be excited about their success. You need to be happy to see them get promoted and pleased to give them raises. You need to love to give bonuses. Basically, you need what we call the generosity gene. It's absolutely critical."

"Don't worry, we will do this." I could sense others around me needed to know our task was not insurmountable. These words have often come during times when I have led fundraising initiatives, particularly capital campaigns. For me, capital campaigns have been exciting and rewarding because the end result is tangible. The end result can be seen. But the task of raising millions of dollars can be daunting. As in any other stretch goal, reassurance comes from displaying visible enthusiasm, conveying your belief in the need and demonstrating your passion. This gives others a boost of confidence to achieve positive results by transforming their mindset. I have often recited a story I once heard about achieving a fundraising goal. A pastor wanted to build a new church and mentioned this goal to a friend. "I need ten million dollars to build a new church, but I don't have any money." His friend replied, "That's easy. Ask someone to donate the ten million dollars." The pastor said, "But I don't know anyone who can donate ten million dollars." His friend answered, "That's easy. Ask ten people to each donate one million dollars." You know what followed. His friend transformed his way of thinking about how to achieve his goal. He helped him understand that his goal was not insurmountable, it just required the support of others and a plan. Perhaps it required asking one hundred people to each give one hundred thousand dollars. The point is, by breaking down the goal and reassuring the pastor that his goal was attainable, the friend motivated the pastor into action and the church was built. He offered solutions and provided the cheerleading he needed.

Transformational leaders champion and inspire others. Let those around you know that you believe in them. My husband Lowell would often facetiously say, "Whatever you're doing wrong, keep doing it!" That was his way of saying, "I'm giving you the big three: responsibility, authority and accountability. Keep doing what you're doing because you're doing it successfully." Help others realize that responsibility and authority go hand in hand. Encourage them to take charge and remind them to always do what is right. Allow others to be empowered – allow others to make decisions. Creating an atmosphere that encourages your colleagues to grow enables your organization to grow.

Give others the freedom to take risks. People can transform themselves and the process begins with empowerment.

Sam Walton, Walmart founder, was quoted by author John Maxwell, "Outstanding leaders go out of their way to boost the self-esteem of their personnel. If people believe in themselves, it's amazing what they can accomplish." It was during my second career, nearly ten years at Eastman Kodak Company, that I realized I had a Sam Walton in my life. He was a regional manager who relentlessly told me that he wanted to see me at 21 Club. His belief in me came in simple snippets on the rare occasions when I would see him during regional sales meetings. He would seek me out, ask how I was and then tell me I had what it takes to be the best. To explain, 21 Club was an annual incentive trip held for the marketing representatives who earned 210 percent of their sales goal. His advice to our entire team was simple: "Whenever I was tired or beat down, no matter how late it was in the afternoon, I would tell myself, 'just one more,' and I would make just one more sales call." I followed his advice. I made "just one more call." At the end of the year I was able to pack my bags for Maui and enjoy 21 Club.

"When people are surrounded by positive energy and positive reinforcement, they feel empowered. They try new things, offer ideas, exude positive energy, and cooperate with their colleagues instead of surreptitiously attempting to bring them down," says Jack Welch. Be tremendously positive when you see your associates and colleagues. When you answer their phone calls, let them hear your positive energy through the phone. When you pass people in the hallways, enthusiastically greet them. When you walk into meetings, make a positive impact on the atmosphere in the room. My husband started his sales meetings each month with, "How's everybody doing?" The typical reply was a boisterous "Great!" because a previous diatribe had informed them that a reply like "Fine" or "Good" or "OK" communicated a lack of enthusiasm in contrast to an energetic, positive response such as "Great!" or "Fantastic!" or "Outstanding!" We have all felt the gloom or negativity created by a halfhearted greeting. It dampens the positivity in a room. It is deflating.

A leader creates an environment for success. Author John Maxwell reminds us that there are three ways in which great leaders excel as people developers. First, they give of themselves. You can impress people at a distance, but you can only impact them up close. Second, they give others an opportunity for ownership as a significant contributor. Third, they give them every chance to succeed. Excellent leaders provide their associates with a compelling vision to work toward, the right tools and training and a positive, creative and encouraging atmosphere in which to work. My husband has always been my cheerleader. Whether I was repairing something around the house or completing graduate school, his words of encouragement have made a huge difference to me. Know who you can count on as your cheerleaders. As Roni Beth Tower said in *Psychology Today*, "It was love made useful." Supporting the dreams of others can be a significant and valuable form of cheerleading.

When someone shares their aspirations with you, offer encouragement and demonstrate through your actions that you believe in them and that you believe they can achieve their goals. My husband often recalls the impact it made on him in high school to see his father at every one of his football games. He would look up in the stands and see his father sitting in the same seat, wearing the school colors and cheering for him and his team. He gave Lowell all he could. We still laugh and repeat his father's constant cheer, "Go get 'em, tiger!" Nearly half a century later, my husband continues to remember how his father made him feel.

A conversation, even a simple reply to someone who shares their ambitions with you, can provide the confidence they need to pursue their dreams. You may not even realize the effect your responses may have. As I passed by the home of my friend's parents, I noticed someone in the garage. It was her father, a retired university science professor.

Although they had moved to Florida to be closer to their daughter, the father remained on the faculty to support his doctoral candidates in pursuit of their degrees. He was one of the smartest men I had ever met, and I trusted his judgment. Seeing him outside, I quickly pulled into their driveway. I shared with him that I was thinking about going back to graduate school to obtain my master's degree. I had been contemplating it for years, and in fact it had been on the list of "my one thing" for quite a while. Without hesitation he encouraged me to apply and went on to say that he was sure I would be accepted. That had been my fear. I was so nervous that my attempt at admission and acceptance would fail. Cheerleading comes in many forms and can be as simple as a nudge from a caring person like the one I received that day.

You can support the dreams of others in many ways. A parent who takes their son or daughter to swimming lessons is supporting their child's dream of becoming a member of the Olympic swim team. A spouse who encourages the other to pursue their writing interests may buy them a desk or office supplies. These implicit ways of cheering others on acknowledges your belief in them. As their cheerleader, simply being present can communicate the loving response that their dream is important – and that you believe their dream is achievable. Being there for them communicates that they and their dreams are important to you and a priority. Our lives can be hectic as we juggle many demands on our time, yet we remember the people in our lives who reprioritized their time to be there for us as we worked toward achieving our dreams. I recall several speaking engagements, particularly acceptance speeches, where I could see the smiles of family members and friends, cheering me on with every grin. Without a doubt, my husband was always in the audience and has always affirmed me, cheering me on with just his presence. Being present at important milestone events reinforces your belief in someone.

Author John Maxwell defines the three areas of support we need in order to maintain the courage required to push forward from "just good enough" to "the best we can be." First, you need cheerleaders in your life. "Spend time with one or two people who believe in you and in your ability to grow. It will do wonders for your courage." Second, seek encouraging environments. Spend time in places where growth, learning, development and achieving goals is embraced. Ensure that you are providing an environment in your organization that encourages individuals to pursue their goals. Surround yourself professionally and socially with others who do the same for you. Spend time with people who encourage each other. Third, boost your courage by gathering encouraging words and positive thoughts from a wide variety of sources including books, seminars and podcasts. Maxwell learned a lesson from his father, who later in life stated, "I have to keep working on my thought life." Your thought life is a product of all that influences you, and you have the ability to harness positivity and motivation by surrounding yourself with encouragement.

Ensure Your Presence is Positive
*"Leadership is about making others better
as a result of your presence and
making sure that impact lasts in your absence."*
Sheryl Sandberg

Be the energy and positive spirit in the room and in your community. Positivity creates more positivity. We rub off on each other. It begins with an enthusiastic greeting. Our positivity can set the tone in an organization, in a meeting or at an event. You can begin the spread of positivity with this simple gesture: smile and wave. It is the universal language of welcome and acceptance.

Lowell and I drove through a cemetery while vacationing. It was common for us to do that. The cemetery was old and beautiful. Large sweeping trees lined the winding roads. We appreciated many of the details evident in the owner's care. But as we slowly drove through the property, each time we came within eyesight of grounds staff, they stopped and glared at us. Their stares communicated to us that we were not welcome. This affected how we felt about the cemetery owners and the entire organization. When we returned home, we recognized that we might possibly communicate a similar message in our own properties. We immediately created a banner, hung it outside our groundskeeper's maintenance area and held a team meeting to explain what we had experienced. We announced our plan to ensure we were not making the same mistake. Our banner said, "Smile and wave every time!" We described our experience to our staff. We shared with them how badly the staff in the other cemetery made us feel. We explained how unwelcomed we felt. Making everyone feel welcome became our mantra from that day forward – a simple gesture to communicate to families that we were glad they had come and that we were there if they needed us. Our experience reminded us that we can set the tone for the atmosphere in a room, in our organization and on the grounds of our cemetery. John D. Rockefeller, who was once the richest person in the world, said, "I would pay more for the ability to deal with people than any other ability under the sun." I believe that dealing effectively with people starts with a smile and a warm, welcoming greeting.

Positivity is a way to help influence another person's success. My husband often comments that I never allow my birthday or anniversary to sneak up on him, that I always help him succeed in remembering those special occasions. "Nancy reminds me of special days so that she is sure to get a present," he jokes. Well, that may be partially true. However, the reality is, I don't want him to forget so I help him succeed in remembering. I enjoy celebrating those milestones, so why not help him be successful? Why not help him remember? In this example, we both win.

Positive individuals focus on what we must do to overcome hurdles. We are problem solvers. We think positively by focusing on what we must do to be successful, not what could go wrong. When things do go wrong, we focus on what we have learned from the experience to help us continue to improve. We understand that failure is essential to growth and an opportunity to learn. Bad things can happen to anyone. The difference between a positive person and a negative one is not the event that happened to us, but how we respond to it. On more than one occasion, I have thought to myself, "I'm glad that happened, now I know what to do when this goes wrong."

Demonstrate your ability to be a difference-maker. The British Royal Navy drew on 400 years of experience and researched a "framework for success" with the goal of establishing "the characteristics that could predict superior leadership." The study revealed that the leadership characteristics exhibited by successful masters and commanders were cheerfulness and effective storytelling. They had positive communication (storytelling) skills. The hallmarks of effective leaders were the ability to influence people through positivity and the interpersonal sensitivity to work with a variety of people. I remember appealing to my Kodak manager for help whenever I had an opportunity to land a large, complicated sale. He would carve out time for me to help with the proposal. When we sat down, the first thing he said was, "This is going to be fun!" Years later, I do not remember the client, the proposal or even the outcome. But I do remember the single most important lesson I learned from him – the positive and enthusiastic inspiration I felt from his approach.

The Center for Creative Leadership studied executives and determined they shared four traits that gained the respect and admiration of others they inspired. These leaders were 1) approachable (they smiled and greeted others), 2) they were calm and confident rather than moody and volatile, 3) they admitted their mistakes and accepted the consequences rather than blaming others, and 4) they were able to get along with a wide variety of people. Leaders such as these have strong interpersonal skills, sensitivity to others and tact. Leaders who are respected and admired exude positivity, have a steadfast calmness and are fair, thoughtful and kind.

Author and professor, Barbara Fredrickson, agrees. In her book *Positivity* she says, "Leaders who cultivate positivity have the chance to tip the scale from narrow, negative thinking to foster broad, innovative thinking and resiliency. This has enormous implications for the productivity of your teams and organizations." Her research shows that positivity requires that you experience and cultivate ten emotions and patterns of thinking: *joy, gratitude, serenity, interest, hope, pride, amusement, inspiration, awe and love.* The result – increased positivity – impacts your feelings and your mindset. Positivity widens the span of possibilities you envision. It brings out the best in you because it builds your resistance to setbacks. And positivity feels good. As Fredrickson says, "The sparkle of good feelings makes you want more, creating motivation to change. But the good feeling is just the beginning."

Did my manager at Kodak know the perfect strategy to formulate a winning proposal? Maybe not. But through his leadership, I was *inspired* to work hard, I took *pride* in doing my best, I became *interested* in learning how to create an effective proposal, and I was *amused* by his witty sense of humor.

Positivity can be supported or derailed by social media platforms. Stories shared are largely about our personal lives. Focus on your messages. Do they make others smile? Do they praise someone else's efforts? If we all tried to fill them with joy, inspiration and gratitude – imagine the impact. Hide the posts and unfollow the people or places that cause negative distractions in your life. Facebook and Instagram, for me, are tools to positively connect – split seconds of joy when I glimpse a friend's trip to the beach with her children or the scenes of a girlfriend's special moments as she and her husband enjoy an anniversary trip. They are moments to praise and provide positive reinforcement for a job well done. They are joyful opportunities to share, to connect, to applaud, to congratulate. Even digitally, we can spread our positivity.

Be with Positive People

> *"Surround yourself with people that reflect who you want to be and how you want to feel – energies are contagious."*
> Rachel Wolchin

I believe we must choose wisely the people we associate with and do our best to avoid the negative people in our lives. Resisting negative influence helps keep our attitude positive. Always try to steer clear of those around you who are nay-sayers. Toxic people are those who are always complaining, procrastinating or making excuses. Negativity is destructive and dangerous to your health. Negativity can sway your thoughts and your emotions.

Negativity can trigger unhealthy responses such as resentment, jealousy, anger or guilt. Next time you are in a group setting, notice the most positive people in the room. Who are the positive contributors? Whose light is beaming? At the next meeting, sit by them. Choose to surround yourself with people who aspire to achieve great things and who are inspiring to those around them.

Be gentle with friends and family but ask yourself whether you come away feeling better or worse about yourself after spending time with each of them. If the answer is that you feel worse after nearly every conversation with someone, spend less time with them, even if they are family. They are affecting your vitality. True friends, spouses and family members should bring each other joy, not hostility and stress.

Name a friend you greatly admire. Write one word describing what is most admirable about him or her. Does the word used to describe them fall into the category of attitude, looks or skill? Most likely it is attitude, and many times that attitude is positivity. It is how they make you feel that makes you admire them so much and makes them such a special friend.

I remember my husband Lowell sharing with another member of his family that they needed to "circle the wagons." He was describing how, once we have our own families, we need to remember that our immediate family unit is what matters most. Our focus must be on our partner/spouse and our children, first and foremost. Our marriage isn't with the entire family, our marriage is with our spouse/partner. Allowing extended family to intrude, allowing them to demand our time or insist we do something or live a certain way can cause a great deal of harm to us and our partner/spouse. Not circling the wagons can often be, in large part, the reason why a marriage fails.

Keep in check another negative force – worry. Worrying is internal negativity. It is the creation of negative thoughts. Positivity is not demonstrated by worry. In her book *Things I Want My Daughters to Know: A Small Book About the Big Issues in Life*, interior designer and lifestyle philosopher Alexandra Stoddard describes how some people mistakenly believe that worrying is a kind of preemptive action. On the contrary, "When we worry, we become troubled and anxious; we have a nagging, a concern, an uneasiness. Worrying won't help you succeed." Worrying can leave us paralyzed with fear.

When you find yourself worrying, try to pinpoint the reason for it. Once you have identified exactly what is bothering you, determine whether there is anything you can do about it. If there is not, try to refocus your energy with encouraging thoughts that lead to positive action. Make a conscious decision to elevate your mood. If there *is* something you can do about your concern, tackle the situation sooner rather than later. Be proactive. Moving forward and implementing a solution will help alleviate your worry.

Motivate and Inspire
"Try to be a rainbow in someone's cloud."
Maya Angelou

"In today's tough economy, should leaders be dogged, analytic, and organized or should they be empathic, charismatic, and communicative? The answer is simple: they need all those traits. ... Leaders need to confidently deliver tough messages with analytics as evidence, but they also need to be sensitive to how people receive those messages," according to *Harvard Business Review's Management Tips*.

A woman who excelled as a manager of a convenience store reported sales that were consistently much higher than other nearby stores in the same chain. When asked how she accomplished this feat, she responded that she found ways – daily – to motivate her associates. She worked at inspiring them to take pride in their work even though many of their jobs were monotonous or routine such as stocking shelves, working as cashiers and assisting customers with the location of specific items. Unlike tasks, she said, people are never done. That was an "aha" moment for me. People are never done.

Like me, you may want things to be done – including people. A task-oriented perspective results in the desire to see projects completed. To make matters worse, you may teeter on the edge of perfectionism – you want things to be done on time and done right. Worse yet, you grew up hearing and *believing*, "If you want a job done right, do it yourself." So, not only do you want it done now and done right, you also want it done *your* way. When you catch yourself in this situation, practice delegating. Empower those around you to grow and to enjoy the challenge of troubleshooting and problem-solving. Allow others to perform. Let them own a project. Provide questions that give them an opportunity to evaluate and modify their plan and determine how they will achieve a positive outcome. As my husband reminds me faithfully, "If someone can do something almost as well as I can do it, and I do it anyway, I have taken two steps backward."

The people who make a difference in your life are not the ones with the most credentials, the most money or the most awards. They are the ones who motivate and inspire you, who care deeply for you and continually invest in you, even if you are never done. Who in this world can you inspire? Perhaps it is your children, a niece or nephew, a friend or a colleague. Everyone can be a difference maker to someone.

Mentoring Successfully

"If you are planning for a year, grow rice.
If you are planning for twenty years, grow trees.
And if you are planning for centuries,
grow women (and men)."
Chinese Proverb

Mentorships are critical to the leadership development of others, particularly those who have been marginalized such as women and members of racial or ethnic minority groups. Be alert to mentorship opportunities in all professional relationships. Be open to becoming a mentor, for the experience is beneficial for your organization as well as for you personally. Influence, involvement, improvement and impact are core principles of the mentor-mentee relationship. Both mentors and mentees gain from a gratifying and worthwhile relationship.

For young professionals to reach their highest levels of achievement, these talented individuals need mentors. Mentorships are crucial for career progression and the relationship can be a win-win. Mentees need knowledge and information, advice on career decisions and access to resources.

Mentors often discover useful information from mentees, such as fresh perspectives that differ from their own. We all grow from the experience. I vividly remember my fourth-grade teacher. I wanted to be just like her. She was a combination of singer Julie Andrews and children's author Beverly Cleary. She liked me. She believed in me. I still have my fourth-grade art project that illustrated "what I imagine" when I hear the Beatles song *Lucy in the Sky with Diamonds*. That day was an exhilarating day in fourth grade! She was my mentor. She did not know it. I did not know it. But she thought I was a 10 on a scale of 1 to 10. She listened when I told her the type of art experiences I would like to have and that I wanted to paint what I was envisioning in my mind when I listened to music. It became a class project. In turn, I could not do enough to be a good student for her. I gave her my full attention, my full effort and my full respect. The relationship, even as a fourth-grader to a teacher, was reciprocal.

Mentoring is a means of developing human resources. You guide others in their quest for growth through learning, self-discovery and personal development, which provides opportunities for fulfillment and achievement. It is a fundamental form of human development in which one person invests time, energy and personal know-how to facilitate the growth and ability of another person. Through mentoring, your own journey becomes more focused. It becomes clearer through the natural reflection process that occurs during dialogue and conversation. Serving as a mentor creates a sense of fulfillment and pride in helping an aspiring professional.

Both mentors and mentees gain from the reciprocal nature of the relationship. The rewarding experience also transcends the relationship when mentors realize they are helping the growth and success of their organizations by professionally developing the associates around them.

One effective way to mentor is coaching. Valorie Burton, author of *Successful Women Think Differently: 9 Habits to Make You Happier, Healthier, and More Resilient,* describes coaching as "the process of asking thought-provoking questions and providing a safe space to explore the answers, empowering a person to take action, learn, grow and ultimately get moving toward their destination."

This insight became clear to me when I sought the advice of my mentor regarding a struggling sales representative on my team at Kodak. His answer surprised me. He said, "It's easy to fire someone. You just do it. The harder but far more rewarding thing to do is to help them be successful." In other words, accepting the challenge and responsibility of mentoring someone to help them succeed is a serious pledge of time and energy. He went on to describe that on a scale of 1 to 10 in achieving the requirements of a company position, if someone has a great attitude and a great personality but is performing in their role at a level 5 or 6, work with them and help them improve. Help them reach level 8 or 9 on the scale of contribution and achievement.

In John Maxwell's book *Mentoring 101*, he says, "Put fuel in their tank." In other words, share the tools that have helped make you successful. Did you read a good book? Share it. Did you watch an excellent YouTube video? Share it. Did you attend an effective presentation? Share your insights. I have often given other women copies of the book *Lean In: Women, Work, and the Will to Lead* by Facebook executive Sheryl Sandberg. I encourage everyone to read it. It was a book I did not pick up or peruse for years even though I saw multiple copies on shelves in bookstores and on tables at airports. Everywhere I went, I saw it. But I thought to myself, "I don't need to read this. What would I have in common with a woman who makes millions a year, graduated from Harvard and is raising two young children?" But then I read it. It was a game changer. Ever since then, I have either bought it for or asked every bright young woman I know to read it.

Mentors initiate a learning process for mentees. You promote intentional learning through coaching, modeling and sharing your own experiences such as anecdotes from your personal journey. You stimulate individual growth by encouraging thought-provoking opportunities to develop a personal vision. You help mentees identify goals and develop winning strategies. As a mentor, you can open doors to learning opportunities and provide a mentee with exposure to broad networks and broader views.

A benefit of mentoring is that the deliberate, intentional thoughtfulness of mentoring forces you as a mentor to take inventory. Are you practicing what you are sharing with your mentee? Does your walk match your talk? In their book *One Minute Mentoring: How to Find and Work with a Mentor and Why You'll Benefit from Being One*, Ken Blanchard and Claire Diaz-Ortiz discuss the elements that mentors and mentees look for in a mentor-mentee relationship. That decision to enter into a mentor-mentee relationship will be based on essence and form. Essence is defined as your value system, what is in your heart. Determine whether you and your mentee have similar personalities and whether your core values align. Form comes after essence. Form is the relationship structure that works for both of you and that logistically fits your respective schedules.

You will be most effective as a mentor if you initiate, facilitate and maintain a rewarding relationship with the person you are mentoring, whether it is formal or informal. First and foremost, get to know the other person – find commonalities and share personal interests and hobbies. In a more formal mentor-mentee relationship, discuss availability, approachability, work styles and boundaries. Discuss the ways in which you prefer to communicate. Perhaps text messages are fine with one person but may seem inappropriate to the other. Agree on when you will communicate and how. Will you meet in person? How often? Ask the mentee to share what he or she hopes to gain from the relationship. It is important that you discuss your mutual expectations. Once you identify the ways in which a mentee feels you could assist them, it is important to determine how you will formally or informally assess the effectiveness of your relationship. Are you providing the level of engagement, coaching and/or guidance the mentee is hoping to receive? Establishing these guidelines will enhance your mentoring relationship and ultimately advance the personal and professional development of the mentee.

Embrace Assistance
"Raise your hand and ask for help,
regardless of what anyone else thinks about it."
Rachel Hollis

You don't need to go it alone. Andrew Carnegie said, "It marks a big step in your development when you come to realize that other people can help you do a better job than you could do alone." Achieving pinnacles in our lifetime cannot be done in isolation.

In their book *The Power of Nice: How to Conquer the Business World*, Linda Kaplan Thaler and Robin Koval remind us how difficult we make our lives if we live by the motto of "fake it till you make it." Thaler overheard her business partner Koval say to her employees, "Ask me for help when I can still help. I will never criticize an employee who comes to me and says, 'I don't know how to do this' or 'I feel over my head.' But if someone waits until it is 24 hours before the client meeting and then says that they did not have enough time, then all we can do is cry over it together."

My sisters have both been remarkable, devoted mothers. They realized that "every-day-parenting" was critically important, recognizing that they led their children by example in the way they lived. My younger sister Carolyn, a stay-at-home mom, was committed to helping her two daughters succeed in their studies. My sisters and I learned the value of an education from our mother, an elementary school teacher. She devoted her professional life to helping children learn. She was particularly fond of teaching them to excel in reading and develop a love of reading. She, herself, was a lifelong learner and avid reader.

When her daughters were in elementary school, Carolyn returned to college and earned a degree in elementary education. Our mother was elated to see Carolyn following in her footsteps. I can remember the joy I heard in our mother's voice when I would call her. Carolyn would periodically ask our mom to review her term papers. Our mother happily shared with me that she was busy helping Carolyn, providing feedback on a paper before it was turned in for grading. It meant so much to her that Carolyn had reached out for this assistance. Nothing could have pleased her more. Embracing assistance allows others to reinforce their love and genuine interest in your well-being by providing aid and support. Requesting help and asking for expertise is complimentary. It affirms that you recognize someone's knowledge and proficiency.

Positive relationships form a personal and enduring community of family, friends, colleagues and neighbors, according to author Valorie Burton. These are informal relationships that include casual conversation. But they are also a source of strength, guidance and support. You can ask these trusted individuals about the best decisions they ever made, the worst decisions they have made and what they would do differently. It gives you an opportunity to reflect on your own decision-making.

Creating a community that encourages you, challenges you, tells you when to pick yourself up and is there when you need them is an important step in a successful journey. Your community includes those you deeply care about and who deeply care about you. Within your community others have strengths you do not possess. Allow yourself the grace to accept help from those who have strengths where you are weak and show gratitude for it.

Every successful person has had to ask for help. They have asked questions. Every person you admire has had their share of failures and have sought and accepted advice from others. We all experience failure; we all make mistakes. "The beauty is in the recovery," according to Emily Ley, author of *Grace, Not Perfection: Embracing Simplicity, Celebrating Joy*. Focus on how you can pick yourself up, continue your journey and handle adversity with grace the next time it happens.

One of my best friends and I serve together on a board of a local nonprofit organization whose mission includes the oversight of a beautiful urban garden as well as an art museum. We both agreed that our organization should be represented by a float in our hometown holiday parade. After parade entrants are judged, awards are presented to the top three participants. We decided we should make a replica of the gardens because they are a lovely and colorful asset cherished by our community. I contacted a colleague from the funeral industry in Michigan. Their company had participated in our industry's national trade show as an exhibitor. Within their trade show booth were a half-dozen women wearing gigantic flower faces that were four feet in diameter and glowing in various vibrant colors. They were imaginative and eye catching. I thought they would be perfect for our float. When I contacted the Michigan-based company, they were delighted to help and allowed me to borrow the flowers at no charge. In fact, they even shipped them and sent return shipping labels as well. It was unexpected generosity – a random act of kindness.

My girlfriend's husband practically halted his electrical business to create our float. It was beautiful and we were all so excited and proud. A first-place victory was in our sights. It was fun to be playful. If you ever want to go back in time and feel like a kid again, ride on a parade float. Although we did not take first place, we enjoyed the experience tremendously, so we vowed to do it again the following year and expand our flower base. Luckily, we discovered a tag on the backside of one of the flowers that divulged the name of the floral designer. The creator was a theatrical and costume designer and seamstress. I contacted her and persuaded her to create fourteen flowers and four smaller versions for children or grandchildren to enhance our art museum and garden promotional efforts.

When the flowers arrived, I discovered they were not functional. They could not be worn. They were missing the critical band that fastens around a person's head, enabling the flower to stay in place. I contacted the designer and explained my plight. She sent the necessary materials and a written note outlining the steps we needed to take to finish the job. I was overwhelmed. The flowers sat on a table in our garage for eight weeks. How could I possibly sew eighteen flower bands attaching the elastic while somehow camouflaging the band beneath the flower petals? It would take hours, and that was assuming I could figure out how to do it. I shared my anxiety with my niece, and she could hear the distress in my voice. She suggested I get help. Of course, I thought, embrace assistance. There was no need to feel I had to go it alone. She was right. I reached out first to the friend I mentioned earlier, who had equally embraced creating a colorful float. She is artistic, creative and talented. She had the strengths and talent I was missing. We quickly assembled a team of six women who came to my home for several hours on a Sunday to complete the task. As it turned out, we had to collaborate as a group on how to affix the headbands and it was much trickier than I had envisioned. It would have been awful to have tried it by myself and would have taken hours. Moreover, who knows if I could have determined the best plan? Without the ability to brainstorm with others and allow them to help solve the dilemma, those flowers would still be in my garage. The advantage was not just in our collective effort, but in utilizing the expertise of others. My friends had brought with them their sewing and crafting backgrounds, plus their wisdom, resourcefulness and expertise. This project also created a bond between us and the cherished memory of a convivial Sunday afternoon. The big takeaway was that I went from a paralyzed position of doing nothing, overwhelmed by the task at hand, to completing it swiftly with the help and laughter of friends.

Make Others Feel Special

"The worst part of success is trying
to find someone who is happy for you."
Bette Midler

Here is some advice I heard long ago: "Imagine there is a sign on everyone that says, 'Make me feel special.'" Longtime CBS newsman Bob Schieffer, who has met many national and international political figures, recounts in his book *This Just In: What I Couldn't Tell You on TV* his initial impression of President Bill Clinton. "When he shook my hand, he held it just an instant longer than a person normally would and made eye contact just a second longer than someone you meet usually does. It made me feel like I was the most important person in the room." It was the same impression diplomat and socialite Pamela Harriman had shared about Clinton.

Effective leaders develop strong personal connections with the people they meet. Remember, good eye contact and the effort to truly engage with another person can leave a lasting, positive impression. Establishing rapport begins with displaying genuine interest in another person. In addition to strong eye contact, a good way to show your interest is by repeating their name back to them followed by a question. The conversation can start with a basic question such as, "How are you enjoying the evening, Mary?"

I attended a multi-day conference with a colleague. We were both looking forward to an evening dinner with another industry colleague. When we planned to meet, he asked if he could bring along a new friend. I was looking forward to seeing my old friend and enjoying a lovely dinner. But it was not the joyful experience I had expected. I realized partway through the evening that our dinner conversation revolved around our friend telling us about his guest. His guest chimed in to add to the stories. We also contributed with questions or comments to show a thoughtful level of interest. But there was never any interest shown in either my colleague or myself by his guest – never a question about where we lived, if we were married, if we had families, what we were enjoying about our trip – nothing. I left feeling unvalued. I vowed to remember my experience and to try very hard not to let anyone feel the way I did that evening. It is so important to make others feel welcome and included. Ask questions to draw others into a conversation. Give others an opportunity to share and experience both belonging and inclusivity.

At that same conference, I listened to several

keynote speakers. One speaker was relatively new to the stage and unfortunately it was obvious. His nervousness showed, and the audience could sense his fear. All the while he spoke, I made sure I paid close attention and smiled at him during his entire presentation. Later that day he approached me and shared that my smile gave him a huge boost of confidence while he spoke. I realized my intentional smile came as a natural way to help him because I knew from my own experiences how reassuring a smile in the audience can be. The positive affirmation that a presenter or a person at the dinner table receives from another person is powerful. The next time you sit in a room with a presenter or sit across from a stranger at a dinner table, provide them with a random act of kindness – your smile. Then engage with them. It will make them feel valued and appreciated. It will have an impact on their confidence, and it will give them a sense of belonging.

Chapter 3

Communicate Purposefully

"When we speak, we are afraid our words will not
be heard or welcomed. But when we are silent,
we are still afraid. So, it is better to speak."
Audre Lorde

It's How You Say It

"I need to listen well so that I hear what is not said."
Thuli Madonsela

Tone and voice inflection as well as non-verbal cues are essential to establishing effective communication and ultimately to forming positive relationships. In his book *Trust Me: Four Steps to Authenticity and Charisma,* Harvard professor Nick Morgan states that verbal content in a speech represents only 7 percent of our communication, while vocal content is 38 percent and visual content is 55 percent. This implies that our posture, facial expressions and hand movements overwhelmingly determine how we are perceived and the emotional connection between ourselves and others. This further translates into the appeal, acceptance and the possible bond experienced between the person or audience and us. Think about that: More than 50 percent of what you are communicating to others is what people see you do, not what people hear you say.

As a funeral director, I often wondered if people could see into my heart. How will they know that I really care? How will they know I hurt for them? In my previous careers, measurement of my compassion and empathy had never really come into consideration. As a funeral director, after sharing tender moments with hundreds of families, I knew that it was not what I said that truly mattered. In fact, my words could often discount our relationship. Instead I came to understand that they knew how much I cared by the nonverbal cues that said, "I'll listen while we sit in silence or while you tell me your stories." In his book *The Funeral*, Doug Manning recommends that the best advice to give family and friends is to "hang around, hug them, and hush." Often, I was asked, "What do I say to someone who has lost someone they love?" If the person was at the funeral home for a service, I would tell them they did not need to find the perfect words to comfort others – their presence was all that was needed. I did, however, often hear words that I did not believe were helpful and may have contradicted the nonverbal, supportive cues. I have heard on occasion comments such as "Get ahold of yourself" or "Don't cry – be strong." So remember, eye contact, nods, smiles and open arms are gestures that welcome, affirm and validate. These are the most helpful. Simply be present. Simply listen.

During my funeral service career, I became active in our national (international) trade association and subsequently served on the board, first as an officer and ultimately as the president. During the year I was president, I was asked to attend the 25th celebration of the Latin American Association of Cemeteries and Funeral Services (ALPAR), held in Colombia, South America. I was asked to provide a short congratulatory speech. I am limited to the English language, so it was a daunting task. But I was determined to deliver my message in their country's first language, Spanish. I wrote a brief, positive message that an associate on our staff, raised in Peru, helped to translate. She and I rewrote the Spanish words phonetically and I practiced reading it aloud. Then we practiced it again and again so that she could help me with pronunciation. I delivered my speech to a crowd of 300 on an outdoor terrace against the dramatic backdrop of the illuminated Castillo San Felipe de Barajas, the fortress in the city of Cartagena. I recited my speech and sensed the audience was aware of my obvious discomfort throughout those long three minutes until I concluded with an enthusiastic "Phew! Gracias!" My smile communicated joy, relief and the exhilaration that comes from achievement. It immediately created a relationship with the audience who shared in my excitement (and my relief). The words in my speech merely set the stage for the warm bonds of friendships that were instantly forged in that moment.

Remember Your Manners

"Good manners reflect something from inside –
an innate sense of consideration for others
and respect for self."
Emily Post

Saying "please" and "thank you" go a long way. Being kind and courteous in your daily life can have a positive effect on your family, friends and associates. Saying thank you shows respect and appreciation for others. The flip side is that you may be perceived as rude and ungrateful when you neglect to use these words.

This basic etiquette is often overlooked. I have witnessed people who seem oblivious to their bad habit. These magic words may seem to be simple niceties. But they are far more significant. They have an impact on the culture of an organization. Saying please shows a sense of appeal and appreciation, an acknowledgment that you see their response as a win-win and a positive act toward a positive outcome. Saying thank you has a similar result. Thanking someone, especially for a small task, is likely to encourage them to continue to positively participate. Saying thank you shows your appreciation. Appreciation is motivating – and it is the right thing to do.

Your Words Matter

*"The way we talk to our children
becomes their inner voice."*
Peggy O'Mara

Ever feel like the conversation between certain people or within certain groups of people is quickly escalating into an uncomfortable or even hostile situation? You sit and wait for the gauntlet to be dropped – the comment that fuels the fire and triggers an all-out assault of one-liners and zingers. This situation is particularly likely to occur in the highly charged, partisan society we live in, family or no family. The Lohmans, like most families, possess a spectrum of opinions and perspectives. The four of us (Lowell, me, Ty and Victor) were very successful in business together and enjoyed our business life and our family life together. But we knew that when the extended family gathered together it could become uncomfortable and unpleasant with differing opinions and the confidence to share them.

As a family we decided to come up with a

code word that when spoken means "Stop whatever you're saying – now – immediately. You are offending someone." We decided our signal would be "Palm Tree." It was an effective tool, a safe word and a system I believe every Lohman accepted. This kind of "safety valve" alerts the person speaking and everyone around you that you find the content of the conversation inappropriate because you adamantly disagree with what they are espousing.

As a family, we boarded a river boat in Nuremberg, Germany, to cruise the Danube to Budapest, Hungary, for a family milestone: we were celebrating my husband's 70th birthday. The river boat had one table of twelve in a private room, but the river boat crew refused to reserve it for us. Every night, as our family's host, I would position myself with party favors and table décor ready to sprint into the dining room as soon as the doors opened to reserve our table.

The first night of our group dinners that week, I passed around a container of cards; each card held a question. I asked everyone to choose one. Then we circled the table, read our question and answered it. It was so popular that we played our question/answer game every night. That made securing our table of twelve even more important and more special. One evening my question apparently prompted me to tell everyone that some people tend to wave like they are washing a windshield although we look more in command if we simply raise our arm in a wave position and hold it still. I have no scientific research that this is true, but it is something I have observed. I followed my unsolicited advice with, "like Sarah Palin does." While I was simulating this wave, my beautiful cocktail ring flew off my finger and landed in my sister-in-law's water glass. At that very same moment, I heard the entire family shout in unison, "PALM TREE!"

Speak Up

"It took me quite a long time to develop a voice, and now that I have it, I am not going to be silent."
Madeleine Albright

Patti Digh, author of *Life is a Verb: 37 Days to Wake Up, Be Mindful, and Live Intentionally*, shared a story about a class she taught on humor and play as intercultural tools. The conversation turned to humor that ridicules a group, such as Polish jokes or blonde jokes. Class members offered examples of how they were, in effect, condoning the jokes by not speaking out against such humor. Digh continued the story with a response one student offered about a technique she uses in that situation. She responds with, "I don't see the truth in that." It helps her control her reaction yet honors her desire and responsibility to respond in a way that registers her reaction as well as helps her speak her truth. There is integrity in finding ways to speak up that honor your values and encourage others to listen. Defensive, volatile or condescending responses can easily become a distraction from the reflective thinking that helps an individual or a group rethink their thoughtlessness or their biases.

Ever since I was a little girl, I have had a big mouth – literally. Now I call it a big smile. It was especially big when I was in fifth grade and wore braces to correct one exceptionally large, crooked, front tooth. As an adult, albeit with people my age who watched television as children in the early sixties, I would say, "The only person with a bigger smile than me is Mister Ed, the talking horse!" (Mister Ed was a television series from 1961 to 1966.) However, I did not have an exceptionally big voice to go along with my big smile. Although I have a fierce independent streak, I did not use my voice to fight for causes. Until I was 13. During the summer of 1973, my older sister Ann asked me to march with her in an ERA (Equal Rights Amendment) protest. "Equal rights?" I thought, "Of course we should have equal rights!" So I proudly paraded through the grounds of the Ohio State Fair holding my sign and chanting, "E-R-A, E-R-A – It's the American Way!"

The U.S. Congress passed the bill in March 1972 and it was sent to the states for ratification. Ohio had not yet ratified it. Thirty-eight states were needed for it to become part of our country's Constitution. Ultimately Ohio ratified the bill in 1974. It may not have been solely due to our protest, but it felt good to have been a part of the process. As the seven-year time limit for ratification approached in 1979, Congress and President Jimmy Carter controversially extended the deadline by three years. However, no additional states ratified. The bill failed.

It was a valuable lesson: We can use our voices and our actions as tools to help create change. It was also a lesson in taking a chance, seizing an opportunity, getting others to hear us and take us seriously enough to fuel action. Knowing that moments will present themselves in your life to take a stand, speak up and speak out, you need to be ready. You need to prepare yourself. Think about the issues around you that will require you to speak up and speak out, such as offensive jokes, racial slurs and gender-biased comments. I have encountered situations when it was uncomfortable yet critical to speak up and speak out. But I have never regretted it. Articulating your messages with respect and diplomacy when faced with right versus wrong, good versus evil or racially biased versus fair allows you to lead by example. It allows you to keep your integrity intact and live up to your commitment not to condone wrongdoing by saying nothing.

Be the person who will speak up. Promise yourself not to remain silent. Summon your courage. Identify the types of comments that will require you to speak up. Contemplate your responses. Perhaps simply asking, "Why do you feel that way?" may help someone reflect on their own bias. But assuming you know what is in their heart and mind is unfair. The goal is to create a dialogue that is helpful, not hurtful. If you simply label someone or label their comment, a wall goes up and the chance to create a better understanding is lost.

Years after I left my career at Eastman Kodak, I ran into a retired executive from the company on an elevator. Lowell and I were attending a cemetery and funeral industry convention at the newly opened Ritz-Carlton in Sarasota, Florida. In the mere seconds of that elevator ride, my retired colleague said, "Nancy, you always made waves but rode the crests of them. You always spoke up." That was the impression I had left with him years before when we had worked together. I was not afraid to speak up and speak out. I was not afraid to "lean in" as Sheryl Sandberg would say. Evidently those who listened appreciated the way in which I shared messages I felt were important. The elevator door opened, he stepped out and I was left pleasantly surprised.

Cultural shifts and change happen slowly. Be an ally to others by setting an example and inspiring others to do the same. Not speaking up leaves you with a sense of personal disappointment – it is a missed opportunity. Speaking up and speaking out demonstrates your integrity. It demonstrates that your thoughts, words and actions are aligned.

Remember the Sunset Rule

> *"Mistakes are a fact of life. It is the response to error that counts."*
> Nikki Giovanni

Deal with issues immediately, do not allow them to linger. Often ignoring an issue, a customer complaint or an employee concern makes the problem even worse. The lingering problem increases your stress level and, even when you ignore it, subconsciously can weigh you down. Decide to act immediately to rectify issues and concerns. Consider it a must to resolve a situation before the sun sets. Thus, the sunset rule.

As a funeral director, I felt the stress and pressure nearly every day of my professional career to provide the perfect tribute for the family we were serving at the time. I knew every family would have one and *only* one celebration of their loved one's life. We either exceeded their expectations or we did not. I placed tremendous pressure on myself and no doubt it trickled over to our staff. Sometimes things went wrong.

On one occasion, one of our funeral directors had a conflict with a local florist. Florists, as you can imagine, tend to have an intimate relationship with funeral home staff. We work side-by-side coordinating our efforts during those sensitive moments of a family's life. That day one of our directors shared with me that he had really upset one of our local florists. I knew we had to fix it. I knew we needed to apologize. And I knew we needed to do it immediately. But how would she receive us? In my panic, not at all knowing how to resolve the situation amicably, I turned to our funeral director and said, "Come on, we're going to go buy hot fudge sundaes and take them to the florist. Then we're all going to enjoy them together. And then we're going to apologize." Something inside me told me we needed to enjoy something sweet. Something told me that a delightful aspect to our visit was needed. As we walked into her shop, we could see our friend in the back room – visibly angry as she stood arranging another floral bouquet. Hesitantly we tiptoed into her back room. We handed a sundae to her. We took ours out of the bag. Then I said, "Thought we could enjoy these ice cream sundaes while we apologized." I smiled, she smiled. Then we cried. We have remained friends ever since.

The Ritz-Carlton calls this "amazing recovery." I connected immediately with this idea when the concept was presented during a funeral home and cemetery trade association convention keynote address. There, a speaker from the Ritz-Carlton Leadership Center explained how they resolve a problematic situation – an upset, disappointed, frustrated or angry guest. The speaker detailed the process of empowering their associates to create amazing recovery from a situation that did not meet the expectations of the guest. He said, "Sometimes our amazing recovery is so good that we create a guest and fan for life. I almost want things to go wrong, just because we make up for it so well."

Part II
Give Well

Chapter 4

Appreciate

"Appreciation can make a day – even change a life.
Your willingness to put it into words is
all that is necessary."
Margaret Cousins

Tender moments give our lives a deeper meaning. It's easy to be in awe of spectacular things, but it's all the little things that make life special. We simply need to appreciate and cherish them. When we begin to focus with thankfulness on the people, things and experiences that make the sum of our life rich and rewarding, we will be even healthier and happier.

Express Gratitude
"Gratitude is a powerful catalyst for happiness.
It's the spark that lights a fire of joy in your soul."
Amy Collette

Having a grateful nature transcends our entire being. We are happier, more light-hearted and tend to value the treasures life gives us, large or small. Showing our appreciation and expressing gratitude transforms our mood, outlook and even health. When we give thanks and are thanked, those interactions leave us feeling connected, which is important to our well-being.

Studies show that gratitude makes us more resilient. We are more likely to bounce back from loss or trauma. "A grateful stance makes us relatively immune to both fortune and misfortune," according to Robert Emmons, author of the book *Thanks!: How the New Science of Gratitude Can Make You Happier*. Being grateful results in the release of dopamine, a feel-good chemical. The effect: We are all happier and nicer. Emmons discovered scientific proof that people benefit psychologically, physically and interpersonally when they engage in systematically cultivating their sense of gratitude.

Gratitude changes our perspective, and perspective is life-altering. Friends, colleagues and family members can be encouraged by your sense of gratitude just as they can be discouraged by your negativity, ungratefulness or complaining. You can choose whether to focus on all that is wrong – your weaknesses, your mistakes, or those of others – or all that is right. Even when you cannot control the circumstances, you can control and change your perspective.

Over the years, I began to be cognizant of how I learned valuable life lessons from my mistakes. In fact, I actually wondered what my future mistakes would be, when I started a new job or accepted a new position. I looked forward to learning from them so I wouldn't repeat them; after all, there was no way to predict them, especially in a new job. I would say to myself, "I wonder what I'll learn the hard way during the next six months of this new position." Of course, I also learned from observing trial and error by others as well. I found it a valuable tool to share with new associates "what I and others had learned the hard way" so they could avoid experiencing difficult lessons first hand.

Years ago, when I was president of our local Chamber of Commerce, the executive director of the chamber became my mentor. She was a mentor to many people and adored by even more. Our work together developed into a natural friendship and a natural mentor/mentee relationship. I always considered her my safety net. While I was on the podium during a special occasion, she would sneak a note into my hands or whisper in my ear when someone in the room had not previously been recognized. She was always attentive, ensuring our organization was inclusive of everyone. She helped me articulate that message as she quietly and discreetly guided me. She knew if I performed well it helped our entire organization. I am eternally grateful for her. But I did not always have that safety net. I remember, before her tutelage began, I had been needled by a board member of a different organization to change my stance on an issue and support his position. After countless emails and exchanges, I responded with my final rebuttal and ended my email with "enough is enough." Gosh, did I really write that? And, oh, how I regret it. A better person would not have typed those words, and I knew better, or at least I know better now. It is never a good idea to memorialize in writing words we may regret. And no one learns from a person who spews a declarative phrase. I should have written, "The board has reached a majority vote and has concluded we will move forward in this direction. I hope as a valued board member you will support the organization and move forward with us." That mistake has guided me on countless occasions since to respond appropriately.

Every day, practice expressing gratitude and appreciation for what you have and for what you have learned. Gratitude implies a humbleness in ourselves. It is the idea that we would not be where we are without the benefit of someone else's kindness or contribution. Be intentional and reflect on what you are grateful for in that moment. Soon it will become natural. Choose a time of day to identify three things you are grateful for; perhaps it is when you first awake, perhaps it is just as the sun is setting or perhaps it is when you lay your head on your pillow at night. As you deliberately participate in this gratitude challenge, the task becomes easy and you find joy in the abundance of things for which you are grateful. From friendships to hot coffee, to a well-running car, to the flowers you see in a garden, you will gain a new-found appreciation for the things you tend to overlook or take for granted. Even when I go to bed anxious about a commitment on my calendar for the next day, I remind myself how grateful I am for my husband next to me, my dog and cat on the bed with us and the wonderful hot cup of coffee I will enjoy in the morning. We all have so much to be grateful for when we focus on the small joys in life.

This daily exercise helps to focus your thoughts on positive things in your life and creates a sense of appreciation for things you may take for granted. Do this often enough for it to become part of a daily routine. You will no longer dwell on the negative in a situation but go straight to the silver lining.

The Impact of the Thank You Note

"No one writes handwritten notes anymore …
Do it, and watch your relationships grow."
Marsha Egan

Author Robert Emmons said, "Gratitude

doesn't just mean uttering thanks." Gratitude means expressing heartfelt thoughts and loving acts. It means a ritual – a concerted, consistent effort of notice and appreciation. Why do you think the handwritten note still – currently – makes a difference? A heartfelt thank you note honors others and can have a powerful impact on someone. A congratulatory note indicates a person has achieved a milestone that deserves significant accolades. Handwritten notes express genuine sincerity because they require our time, focus and energy in their creation. A study at the University of Texas at Austin revealed that senders of thank you notes expected the notes they had written to generate a happiness rating in their recipients of three on a scale of one to five, with five being the happiest. However, the recipients reported their happiness as a four on average. In other words, thank you notes have a greater impact than we realize. They were not simply thank you notes, but personal expressions of gratitude. The recipients sensed that the notes were a result of having affected their senders in a very positive way. The quality of writing was not a factor, by the way. It was the warmth and genuineness of the notes that mattered to the recipients.

I, too, have appreciated the sincere gesture and personal time that has been invested in a thank you note by the sender. I have also been struck by the number of people who have commented on thank you notes they have received from me. I have noticed that a handwritten thank you note feels more precious to me personally than one that is typed.

Not too long ago, I ran into a colleague of mine from the funeral industry who had resigned from his position years ago. He reminded me of the letter I had sent him at that time and told me how much my note had meant to him. He went on to share that, sadly, he had received only one other note. He said, "Although I didn't request a response nor expect one, it's interesting to me that no one else took the time to reach out. I guess they were all busy – of course, except for you. You really are amazing." What is amazing is how much a written note means to someone.

I have discovered that the right paper, the right pen and the right moment are all critical to the sincerity of a personalized note. They set the stage, so to speak, to give a thank you note the time, authenticity and genuineness it deserves. I have a favorite fountain pen – a Mont Blanc with purple ink cartridges. The pen itself denotes "this is for something special." I use it when I write thank you notes with intention. Choosing the perfect card or *real* stationery and your favorite pen will help you focus on the process for a more eloquent and thoughtful outcome.

I came across an envelope in a file recently. Instantly I knew it was my mother's handwriting.

The envelope alone, addressed to me in her writing, brought me joy. The cadence of her cursive penmanship, the invisible straight line that guided her pen – it was all part of the distinctive handwriting style that defined our rule-abiding, tailored, elementary school teacher of a mom – our smart, educated, witty, resourceful and resilient mom. Whether it is straight or loopy, spidery or bold, your handwriting will be cherished by someone, too. And someone will save one of your notes forever, just like I am saving the note from my mother.

Fill a Gratitude Box

"Gratitude makes sense of our past,
brings peace for today,
and creates a vision for tomorrow."
Melody Beattie

Knowing that a thank you note can make a big impact on another person came from my own realization that many of the handwritten notes I have received changed my life by changing that very moment in my life.

Decades ago, after cremating a family's loved one, the family accused us of not returning to them the correct cremated remains. I knew we had returned the correct ashes, but I also knew that perception is greater than reality. Our employee had accidentally written the incorrect burial transit permit number on their paperwork, a detail that did not need to be written on that particular paperwork in the first place. But that set off a chain of questioning. I did not blame the family for their accusation, but it hurt that they did not believe me and could not see that I was being honest. They did not know that honesty is one of my core values. If that was not bad enough, the family decided to share their grievance publicly – the story made its way into our local newspaper. It was a difficult time.

The names, dates and anguish eventually dissipated, and I have forgotten many of the details, but what I have never forgotten is the card I received the day after the newspaper article ran. It was sent to me by a woman who I socialized with whenever we happened to run into each other. In her letter she expressed her heartfelt sympathy for the pain she knew I was experiencing. She stated her belief in me and that she knew there was "much more to the story." At that moment, she was an angel in my life. Her heartfelt, handwritten note was more appreciated than she will likely ever know, even though I mention it to her nearly every time I see her! She empathized with me and she was there with her support. At that moment, it was her handwritten note that made all the difference.

There have been other times when a handwritten note made a huge impact on my life and was a difference-maker in its encouragement, support and affirmation: Letters that families wrote to us after we cared for their loved one and coordinated the celebration of life services, or notes from strangers thanking us for a donation or support of some kind in our community. Subsequently, I began to save the cards and notes that had such a positive effect on me, and those feelings of affirmation and reassurance come rushing back to me when I re-read them. This is why I encourage you to create a gratitude collection. Choose a box, a pocket file or a drawer in which to save those precious notes. Keep it handy. Every now and again, reach in and take one or two out to re-read. When you need a boost, those cards and letters will be waiting. The note I received from my friend that difficult day was a life saver and remains one of the most treasured notecards in my gratitude box.

Practice Random Acts of Kindness

> *"Carry out a random act of kindness,*
> *with no expectation of reward,*
> *safe in the knowledge that one day*
> *someone might do the same for you."*
> Princess Diana

Selflessness and altruism expressed in a kind or giving act is not altogether selfless. As it turns out, giving to others makes us feel good. The act of giving, and then receiving reciprocal thanks, releases dopamine and serotonin, two crucial neurotransmitters responsible for our emotions. They enhance our mood immediately and make us feel happy. No matter who the person is, no matter how much they have or do not have, your random acts of kindness will have an impact on them and on you. No matter the size of the gesture, you may affect a life more than you know and you positively affect yours as well, even if you are not aware.

When we first moved into our home, we bought a mailbox in the likeness of a manatee. We have adored him for nearly twenty-five years. A few weeks after the manatee had been installed, we noticed a small giftbox in the mailbox. Inside the box was a gold manatee charm. The card read, "Your mailbox brings a smile to our faces every day as we ride by. Thank you. Enjoy this charm as our way of saying thank you. As Oprah says, 'Do random acts of kindness,' and this is ours."

There are many ways to perform random acts of kindness for others. Gifts are not the only way. Seeking to include others in social situations can be one of the kindest things we do. At a recent cocktail party, I was chatting with a small group of people. In my peripheral vision I could see someone standing by herself and I could sense how uncomfortable and awkward she felt. I know because I have felt that same way at times. I immediately interrupted my own story and said, "Please join us,

I think you'll enjoy this story, too." I drew her in. I swung a social life preserver to her and I knew I would have wanted the same done for me. Simply including others in a conversation can be an act of kindness. In social settings, be cognizant of those who are not feeling included. It is one of the nicest random acts of kindness you can provide. Invite others into the conversation so they are not excluded. It costs nothing and can mean so much to others.

Be Generous

> *"No one has ever become poor by giving."*
> Anne Frank

It's known as karma: Do something good and something good will come back to you. For years, my husband and I have tipped generously and have been outspoken to our friends and colleagues about doing the same. Tipping generously won't change your life, but it may make a big difference in the life of the receiver. It stuns me each time I witness someone being less than generous with their tip. How can they rationalize an enjoyable lunch or dinner but not tip well when they have received excellent service? On giving, author Douglas M. Lawson said, "We exist temporarily through what we take, but we live forever through what we give." Remember, not only does a good tip make someone's day, it could even change their life.

Lowell and I have experienced first-hand the difference a generous tip can make. We have tipped taxicab drivers and restaurant servers who have broken down and wept. We have had employees stop in disbelief. We have had store clerks chase after us to thank us after discovering what we had left for them. On a few occasions, individuals have shared with us the impact of our tip. One woman told us that she and her husband along with their three children were living in a one-bedroom hotel room, evicted from their apartment when they fell behind in their rent due to the expense of her cancer treatment. Another woman shared with us through her tears that she could finally afford to fix her car. By tipping generously, we are all making a difference in the world – one person at a time.

Money is not the only way to give. Boosting the morale of others is also a way of giving yourself, your energy and your enthusiasm. It can reap rewards in a domino effect that exponentially affects the world around you. Being generous goes beyond giving gifts or making charitable donations. As author Patti Digh explains, "Generosity, as it turns out, is a way of being in the world, not a way of giving in the world. It has little to do with giving gifts, and everything to do with giving space (and support) to others to be who they are."

In Linda Kaplan Thaler and Robin Koval's book *The Power of Nice: How to Conquer the Business*

World with Kindness, they describe the impact of such simple gestures as waving hello, bringing a gift to a party or clinking glasses in a toast. Although many of these customs originated in communicating that we present no threat, now they demonstrate our good intentions and giving hearts. There are many ways to demonstrate that we "come in peace."

Often, we hear how people choose to give back. We hear how rewarding it feels to them. Giving back through volunteerism or nonprofit organizational leadership, such as serving on a board of directors, may become the outlet you need outside of your professional career. It fills the rest of your cup of life. It can be the facet of your life that provides purposeful and meaningful work.

Many years ago, I applied to participate in our Chamber of Commerce leadership program. It was a great experience that led to lifelong friendships with several community enthusiasts in the class. One of our guest speakers emphasized the importance of accepting and fulfilling the responsibilities required of a board member serving a charitable organization. He said, "Remember the 4 W's and decide the way in which you can contribute." He went on to describe ways to share your time, talent or treasure: Be a worker, a worrier, be wealthy or be wise. As a *worker* you volunteer your time and effort for logistical details that require volunteers and leaders. It may include setting up for events, staffing a registration desk or assisting in other ways with programs or events. You can serve an organization as a *worrier* with expertise in legal or financial matters, such as an accountant or attorney can provide. If you are *wealthy* (or are simply passionate about stretching your level of giving), you can serve by making significant donations and providing additional financial resources to the organization through your sphere of influence. Lastly, you can apply your *wisdom* as a board member who understands an organization's history and can help plan its future effectively based on that perspective and knowledge.

Speaking positively about your community, your company, the organizations you serve and even your family demonstrates the care you have for the greater good outside yourself. That is a contribution. If you are passionate about a cause and choose to become part of an organization to promote its mission, become that organization's ambassador and cheerleader. Have your talking points ready so you can describe the positive impact the organization has in your community.

Chapter 5

Befriend

Nurture Friendships

"Where would you be without friends?
There's nothing like a really loyal,
dependable, good friend. Nothing."
Jennifer Aniston

Giving, loving, caring and sharing are the four beautiful gifts of friendship. Friends inspire us to try new things (like writing a book!), friends encourage us to work toward our goals, friends extend support, compassion and empathy when we are going through a tough time, and they motivate us to have a giving heart. They inspire us to be the best version of ourselves. True friends are those we can count on daily and with whom we naturally invest our time. Our depth of friendship comes only with engagement and a mutual feeling of trust. Genuine friendship is built on honest disclosure, which is not possible without trust. Our good friends are a connection, they tie together our past which they have fully accepted and support us as we move into the future. They help us keep our spirits up when we are experiencing a low point. I have often said, "My friends laugh at my jokes even if they aren't that funny and they commiserate with me and my problems when they're not that bad."

Years ago, I identified with the description of the type of individual who possesses the "connector" trait. Far from being a matchmaker – except when linking up a prospective pet parent with a particular type of dog or cat at our rescue shelter – I relish opportunities to help others connect with one another, particularly when I perceive a real win-win for them through a new professional relationship. I also love bringing friends together, especially those I think would enjoy a new-found friendship if only they were given a chance to get to know each other. Many times, I have met other women and thought, "If we just had more time to be with one another, we could be great friends." I have one dear friend who is also gifted as a connector. Several of my most treasured friendships were established through her introduction. On more than one occasion, she sensed correctly that a friendship would ignite if given the opportunity to spend time together socially. Once we came together and enjoyed a conversation, which covered a variety of subjects, we found common ground and it launched a lasting friendship.

Prioritizing our friendships by investing significant time and energy nurtures those relationships. For decades now, my girlfriends and I have planned an annual holiday shopping spree. Amid sometimes complete holiday chaos, we escape out of town for an all-day excursion. It has become a tradition and one of the most important days of the year for all of us. It is a full day devoted to enjoying a shopping experience together and enjoying each other's company. Anticipation makes the event even more fun, so I send invitations (not that anyone needs a reminder). The day of our trip is enhanced with limousine service, cocktails and small holiday gifts that we exchange. The hour-plus drive back and forth, along with our group luncheon, are special moments of the day when sharing takes place. That is when we all feel connected. Research shows happiness is derived as we interact with friends face to face. That connection activates our endorphins, which make us feel good. A connection with friends on Facebook, Twitter or Instagram does not have the same effect.

Deep, authentic friendships, built by going "through thick or thin" together, require time, transparency and effort. I do not play tennis and rarely eat ice cream sundaes, but oh how I remember the days back in ninth grade when I played tennis with my middle-school best friend. After the game, we would go to Denny's for a hot fudge sundae. Then we would laugh about ordering a Diet Coke to go along with it! She remained a good friend as my teenage life unraveled. My father's alcoholism, my brother's death and our mother's independent new life left me thankful I had my own independence, a defiant ambition with a good deal of resourcefulness and most importantly a wonderful friend in her. For fifty-plus years we have remained friends and we pick up right where we left off each time we reconnect.

Our authentic and loving friends inspire us to persevere. They inspire us to be a positive influence in our community. We can count on them whether we interact daily or once a year. That depth of friendship is only developed with time well-spent together and often through turbulent times. True friendship is an investment. Just as the only way you grow wealth is over time, the same holds true for friendships. They become priceless.

Support Your Friends' Victories

> *"Surround yourself with only people*
> *who are going to lift you higher."*
> Oprah Winfrey

True friends revel in each other's victories. Successful, positive people realize that when a friend accomplishes a goal, there are plenty of "wins" for everyone. Their success does not negate yours. We know that the more everyone achieves, the better our world will be. We know that surrounding ourselves with successful people can teach us, inspire us and motivate us.

I love our sparkling city by the sea, Ormond Beach, Florida. I am grateful for so many aspects of my life and the lives of all who share the common denominator of place, the geographical location we call home. The Intracoastal Waterway runs through our city, and most of the places we travel to – whether it is to the dollar store or a long-distance commute to Ohio – require crossing our city's bridge. The view from the crest of the bridge is stunning, and our sunsets are magnificent. I often hibernate on the weekends, enjoying my staycation overlooking the river. One rainy Saturday morning, just after I had accepted the opportunity to chair the Halifax Humane Society's Capital Campaign to renovate and expand our community's animal shelter, I was watching a video production on YouTube created by an animal shelter. It was accompanied by the ABBA song, *Take a Chance on Me*. It remains one of the funniest and most touching videos I have ever seen – and I cry each time I watch it. Just as I had begun my second or third cry of the morning, our doorbell rang. It was one of my best friends. In my robe, I answered the door with messy hair and my face smeared with tears and mascara. Whatever the reason she came to the door, it was hijacked by my insistence that she join me as a fellow dog lover to watch the video. We cried together. I explained that I had been asked to chair the capital campaign and how thrilled I was to have been selected for the job. She immediately became excited for me. She was so supportive that I asked her to join me as my assistant chair. As a devoted friend, animal lover and pet parent, she not only celebrated my success, she joined me so that we could work together to ensure the project's success. She and her husband assisted with the construction of the animal shelter's new building and they made a generous donation.

Over the course of the five-year project, I felt her support for the incremental goals we achieved as we saw our project to fruition. Then she and I celebrated our success. Author John Maxwell's celebration principle tells us, "The true test of a relationship is not only how loyal we are when friends fail, but how thrilled we are when they succeed. The joy of accomplishment diminishes when no one celebrates with you."

My husband believed the true benefit of a family business was the joy of celebrating accomplishments. When our family purchased a business, achieved a goal or completed a large project, we celebrated together. Even after a particularly stressful day of hard work, we would go out afterward to commemorate "a job well done." Some of my fondest memories from our family business were when the four of us were together after a long day. Lowell shared, "After our family sold a group of the businesses we owned and operated together, I went out on my own. But I realized that when I bought or sold a business, I had no one else who was really excited about it." Make an extra effort to celebrate the successes of your friends, your family and of a job well done.

Enjoy the Holidays

*"Christmas – that magic blanket that wraps
itself about us, that something so intangible
that it is like a fragrance. It may weave a spell of
nostalgia. Christmas may be a day of feasting, or of
prayer, but always it will be a day of remembrance –
a day in which we think of everything
we have ever loved."*
Augusta E. "Gussie" Rundel

For years, I carried a self-imposed expectation that I should be able to enjoy a smorgasbord of holiday traditions and parties while continuing to fulfill life's year-round obligations. Then a friend said to me, "I just let everything else go that, frankly, really could wait, and I enjoy the season." What an "aha" moment for me. I immediately began to cancel appointments that could wait until January and temporarily modified my schedule to accommodate holiday merriment. I reevaluated our holiday traditions, determining which I enjoyed and which I needed to eliminate in order to relish the others. I reduced our holiday decorating to include only the ribbons, wreaths and ornaments that brought me joy and donated the remainder to a charity thrift shop. I made gift-giving and holiday gatherings a priority. I changed my email signature to communicate "I am enjoying the holidays."

Review your calendar and postpone any commitments that are not critically time-sensitive. Reevaluate holiday traditions to determine the preparations and events you want to embrace, those that bring you joy. As for those that are obligatory, burdensome, and stressful – just let them go or reconfigure them. Be honest with yourself and your family. Carve out the time and space you need so you can avoid feeling overtaxed. It is impossible to be fully present in the moment when you are feeling overwhelmed. The moments you want to savor come around only once a year, so limit other commitments where possible.

Experience how you feel when you are intentional about holiday music. Listening to seasonal carols is a tradition many of us grew up anticipating as part of the magic of the season. The first Christmas my husband spent with our family in Ohio opened his eyes to these traditions. Because he was raised in a family of all boys, his mother used to repeatedly echo, "Ball, ball, ball – all my boys ever wanted to do is play ball." When he visited Ohio, he discovered that our holiday traditions were very different from his and included decorating Christmas cookies, baking homemade pies and sorting through holiday cards to enjoy the sentiments from family and friends. Like many families at Christmas, we also enjoyed holiday carols. Our mother would play the piano as we sang along – *Silent Night, Deck the Halls, Jingle Bells* – all the favorites. It was something new for Lowell, but he found it delightful, just as we did. It was foreign and fun to him, quaint and picturesque. Similar to us, I know several families whose holiday traditions also include music. Their traditions include events such as attending a local university choir's Christmas concert, a high school orchestra performance and kicking off the holiday season by watching the famous Macy's Thanksgiving Day parade together while they began preparing their Thanksgiving Day family dinner.

The sounds of the season are nostalgic and can bring us joy. Consider including music in some form in your holiday and continue the tradition by preparing in advance a playlist of holiday music favorites, songs made special to you by the talented singers who recorded them. Choose places to enjoy these favorites in casual ways such as in your car while you run holiday errands or as background music in your home, even perhaps while you shower. For me, no one sings *White Christmas* like Andy

Williams and no one sings *Grown-Up Christmas List* like Amy Grant. These songs remind us that there are positive correlations between the ideals we cherish, internalize and appreciate in others and the holiday carols we gravitate to. Many carols are jolly while others are ballads that express sentimental wishes for harmony and humanity. These holiday ballads remind us to do our part for world peace. They inspire us to extend extra kindness, empathy and compassion. They encourage us to give, not receive, and help us practice deliberate acts of kindness. They inspire simple gestures like baking holiday cookies for an elderly neighbor or delivering holiday gifts to a local children's charity to brighten someone else's day. These gestures increase our holiday enjoyment rather than causing us to feel burdened by it.

I particularly enjoy *There's No Place Like Home for the Holidays*. It reminds us to make our holidays count by connecting with family and friends. The children's favorite, *Rudolph the Red-Nosed Reindeer*, reminds us to support the underdogs around us. Rudolph, an outcast reindeer because of his shiny red nose, was jeered by his fellow reindeer. Remember? They refused to let him join their reindeer games. Then one foggy Christmas eve when a winter blizzard severely reduced visibility, Santa asked Rudolph to guide his sleigh with his bright red, lighted nose. Open yourself to the messages in music that surround us during the holidays and allow it to inspire you.

Keep in mind that holiday traditions should bring you and those you love joy. If a change must be made in a holiday tradition, let it come from a place of love or limitation instead of hurtfulness. Remember, too, that holidays can produce expectations that are placed on us by others. It is important to recognize those expectations and embrace them *only* if you choose to. As an example, I love to send holiday cards. Each year I design them myself along with a one-page photo collage of the most memorable moments of our year. The photos often incorporate groups of friends and feature special events, occasions or places we have traveled during the year. One year, someone mentioned to me how important they felt it was for Christmas card envelopes to be hand-addressed. For years I internalized this expectation and painstakingly spent hours addressing envelopes. Then I stopped one year and reevaluated that aspect of my card tradition. Was it really an expectation of others that I hand-write each envelope? That year, I sent my holiday address list alphabetized in an Excel spreadsheet to my printer and had each envelope beautifully printed by them. I have never looked back. Remember, only embrace the traditions that bring you joy.

The holidays are also a good time to remind yourself and others to embrace diversity, inclusivity and belonging. Teach children to be kind – don't just read Rudolph's story, share with them the lesson of his experience.

Savor the sweet treats of the season, give meaningful gifts, gaze mindfully at holiday lights, hear the messages in holiday music and give thanks. Note: Although I use Christmas as an example of a holiday, be sure to find ways to honor any holiday that holds special meaning for you.

Create Ceremonies and Celebrations
"Celebrate life's special moments!"
Nancy Lohman

The single most important lesson I learned as a funeral professional was from Alan Wolfelt, founder and director of the Center for Loss and Life Transition in Boulder, Colorado. He said, "When words are inadequate, have a ceremony." That is why we have baptisms, weddings, and of course, celebrations of life. When something significant occurs, such as a wedding, the ceremony and celebration are declarations that the event is something very special.

My family and friends have come to expect this of me – the creator of ceremony and celebration. As author John Ortberg encourages, "People who want to pursue joy especially need to practice the discipline of celebration. Find a joy mentor." I consider myself a joy-mentor-hopeful.

One of my joy mentors was my mother-in-law, Opal. She would say, "The anticipation is as much fun as the event!" And we knew that was true because she invested time and effort into every element of a family celebration. She knew the details made the difference. Her Easter celebration was a colorful feast. You could ask anyone in the family and they would recall the annual tradition of a vegetable plate adorned with a garnish in the shape of a palm tree made from a carrot and a green pepper. And they can picture the backyard swing with a garland of pastel flowers wrapped up and down its ropes. Opal also filled her home at Christmas with beauty and grace. Her white Christmas tree stood elegantly in her turquoise living room. And she, too, was full of beauty and grace. I remember the first Christmas with the Lohmans. We walked into Opal's living room where she was standing to greet us – in her red and black sequin outfit. Sequins on Christmas Eve! I was spellbound.

Making moments special does not require sequins, however. It simply requires advance thought, preparation and effort. There are many ways to add to the significance of a holiday event or milestone celebration. One idea is to ask each person to recite what they are most thankful for. Another could be a fun group photo. These are simple and wonderful traditions. To make a celebration even more memorable, introduce some type of detail that speaks to the occasion. I've supplied colorful Santa hats for a Christmas reunion, glittery bunny ears for a family brunch at Easter and red, white and blue scarves to celebrate a patriotic event such as a space launch. While planning funeral services, families shared with me the ways they remembered a loved one, especially during the holidays. Some lit a candle, some had a photo of the deceased where the family gathered, others had an empty chair and place-setting at the table representing their loved one. These signified that someone was missed and remembered. Making moments special can be as simple as a personalized gesture of appreciation and acknowledgment for those present and those we have lost.

Travel traditions can also incorporate ceremony and celebration. Traditions can be anything that make a vacation uniquely yours, creating anticipation and excitement. The ideas are endless. Lowell and I make sure that one photo is taken of the two of us on each trip. It becomes an 8-by-10-inch print we hang in our hallway. We have dozens of framed prints from vacations over the years – a collage of unique trips and special moments. It is a treasured collection that we stop to enjoy regularly, as do our house guests. We have taken several trips where I have had a banner created in advance and tucked away in my suitcase commemorating a significant detail of our trip. For our trip to Antarctica,

I surprised Lowell with a banner we held for the photo we would add to our wall collection, which said "Hi from Antarctica. Bucket List completed – all seven continents!"

My most cherished travel tradition is a tribute to my favorite travel writer. As we near the end of any lengthy vacation, we stop and pose for a photo with our passports. As Erma Bombeck wrote in her hilarious 1991 best-selling book that offers advice for the world-weary traveler, "When You Look Like Your Passport Photo, It's Time to Go Home!"

Give Meaningful Gifts

"Since you get more joy out of giving joy to others, you should put a good deal of thought into the happiness that you are able to give."
Eleanor Roosevelt

We all recognize the excitement we feel when we give someone the perfect gift. It is an intimate, genuine gesture of our love and it is recognized as such by the receiver. My husband received a decanter from one of his college roommates who ultimately grew to be one of his best friends. His wife had engraved on the decanter this inscription: "Roommates by Chance, Friends by Choice, Brothers by Heart." It is not the decanter that makes the gift special, but the message. It is his most treasured gift, a reminder that true friendships are few and far between and should be cherished.

The ideal gift requires active listening. It requires us to be attentive to our friends and family members' interests. It includes reflection on shared experiences. We have all felt what it was like to receive a gift that was "just perfect" for us, whether it represented our favorite color, one of our pets or a wonderful memory of a special experience we shared together with the gift giver. When contemplating a gift, think about the types of gifts you could give family members or friends that would trigger the "how did she/he know?" response.

Lowell and I had the good fortune of enjoying the maiden voyage of the Queen Mary 2 when it set sail on a round-the-world cruise. Yes, just like the movie, the trip was eighty days. Our room was cabin number 9005. I often close my eyes and dream that tapping my heels together could instantly return us to that room. The amazing views from our balcony and the spellbinding itinerary of cities we visited was a dream come true. Our neighbors in cabin number 9007 were from Berlin, Germany. They are two beautiful, generous, interesting, loving people who have become lifelong friends. We see each other at least once a year, and over the years those visits have become very important to us. One year when they came to the United States, they brought with them a miniature Buddy Bear. Buddy Bears are painted, life-size fiberglass bear sculptures developed in Germany by Klaus and Eva Herlitz, in cooperation with sculptor Roman Strobl. The raised arms of the standing Buddy Bears are intended to indicate friendliness and optimism. They have been placed throughout Berlin. Our Buddy Bear is not six feet tall, he is a twelve-inch replica, but what makes him special and a focal point in our home is that he is adorned with photos of the four of us, spanning the years of our friendship. There could not have been a more perfect gift than a personalized minia-ture Berlin Buddy Bear to remind us each and ev-ery day how lucky we are to have these amazing friends in our lives.

Although personalizing every gift isn't prac-tical, I've found that keeping my eyes open through-out the year for items that friends and family mem-bers would love has given me an opportunity to run across the perfect gift more regularly. One of my dear friends reminded me of this as she recited each of our mutual friends' shoe size, their favor-ite color and the things in life they are passionate about. Whether it is mermaids or maltipoos – know-ing their favorite things makes it possible to con-centrate your gift-giving efforts so that your gifts express how much you care. The pricelessness of a gift has nothing to do with the price.

I also recommend that you take a hostess gift whenever you attend a party or a get-together as a gesture of kindness and good manners no matter who your hosts are or how well you know them. Walking in with a gift in hand is the proper way to express your thanks for being included and it will make a difference because it will make your host feel appreciated. One way to always be prepared is to keep on hand universal gifts like wine, champagne or chocolates. Create a specific area in your home to store and organize all the gifts you have purchased for future use.

Joyful gift-giving is one of my top priorities – not necessarily expensive gift-giving, but thoughtful gift-giving. I strive to find gifts that communicate intention. I want to show appreciation through my hostess gifts, I want to show love through gifts to my girlfriends and I want to show gratitude in the thank you gifts I give to those who make my life easier. With our busy lives, it is not always possible to choose the perfect gift for every occasion, which is why I advocate having a ready supply of gifts for the occasions that can quickly sneak up on you. A bottle of quality champagne or wine with a seasonal stopper is a wonderful gift and appreciated by most hosts.

I am amazed at how often my friends give me perfect gifts. From ornaments to lotions to hats to baubles, their gifts cheerfully shout out, "I know you, I like you, I cherish our friendship." I hope I give back to them the same affirmation. Strive to communicate through your gift-giving how much you care.

Be the Keeper of Memories
*"Memories make the good times
happen time and time again."*
Charmers by Hallmark

Shared experiences, significant events and poignant moments are often captured through photos, whether they are taken intentionally with a camera or spontaneously with a smartphone.

When my father-in-law died, my husband said, "I really don't care about anything except the photos." Photos are prized possessions for so many of us and are nearly every home's hidden treasures. Years ago, I discovered that to enjoy our memories through the photos that captured special moments with family members and friends, we needed to be able to physically share them. It was not enough to swipe through our phones trying to find a photo that related to a conversation. So, I began creating digital photobooks and surprising people with the gift of photos in hard copy and in a way that told a story.

As the keeper of memories, I have found that digital books are an easy way to share photos and an enjoyable way to reminisce. Digital scrapbooking allows me to create one book for each year with a page or two for each event, holiday, party or experience that I have captured with photos. And, it allows me to create a commemorative gift for those who shared a special experience such as a holiday, a milestone birthday or a vacation. These projects require keeping photos organized on my computer by year and then subsequently within that file by month and event. A friend of mine creates one of these photobooks each year for each of her children with the focus in their respective books on them. They are treasured keepsakes but a slightly different system than mine, which is fine. It is the system that is important, and it is unique to you. By documenting life, year after year, in photobooks, we can enjoy them frequently and share them digitally. They are also a significant space saver because they are not nearly as cumbersome as traditional photo albums or scrapbooks.

This endeavor is possible only with an excellent, well-organized photo storage system. Again, it is all in the system. You can import all your digital photos from your smartphone and camera into one repository, either on a computer (which requires an external backup for safe-keeping) or with a trusted cloud-storage provider.

Creating video, photo and music tributes to celebrate milestone birthdays or to commemorate a person's life can also be accomplished more easily with an organized archival system. Unfortunately, for some of us, many early photos are stored away in boxes or photo albums. It's a daunting but rewarding task to scan them all so that they are accessible to share.

Being the keeper of memories does not necessarily mean the keeper of memorabilia. Especially over the years, the items can become unmanageable. Reevaluate collectibles whether they are stored or displayed. Are you enjoying them? Do you look at them, touch them or study them? Do you smile when you see them? If so, they are most likely worth keeping. If not, it may be best to find them a new home.

How do you reminisce about the special moments in your life? How do you experience your photos as shared joy with others? Establish a system tailored to the ways you prefer to evoke that joy.

Develop A Happiness Lifestyle

"It's a helluva start, being able to
recognize what makes you happy."
Lucille Ball

A growing study in personal and professional development is Positive Psychology research – the scientific study of "human flourishing" or "what happens when things go right." It is the study of the strengths that enable individuals and communities to thrive. It gives us an understanding of the factors that enable achievement, foster happiness, build courage, strengthen self-esteem and clarify meaning in our lives. Research shows that 50 percent of our happiness and/or joy is genetically set, 10 percent is set by circumstances and 40 percent is influenced by how we manage our thoughts and our intentional activity. According to the Coaching and Positive Psychology Institute, the building blocks of happiness are positive thinking, social connection, managing the negative, living in the moment and achievement (setting and reaching goals).

Happiness, as it turns out, is most often experienced with others when we give our time and talent to helping others or assisting an organization with a mission that resonates with us. According to Robert Lustig, professor emeritus of the University of California at San Francisco, "Pleasure occurs when you get something, such as winning money at a casino. Happiness results from giving our time or money to others or to a charity." The human connection is the difference maker. Happiness is linked with deeds or successes achieved with others or achieved for others. Multiple studies show that contributing to another person or society-at-large boosts good health. It can be as simple as attending someone's graduation or their performance at a concert, recital or sporting event. Contributing to others and/or the greater good makes us feel proud and satisfied, improving our self-worth and self-regard. We feel better physically as well.

We also become happier when we help other people find their happiness. The Dalai Lama says, "If you want to be happy, practice compassion." Helping others makes us happy because it gives us a sense of purpose. In fact, a study from the London School of Economics compared the variance in happiness levels in people who do not help others on a regular basis to the happiness of weekly volunteers. They found that the more we help other people, the happier we are.

When it comes to focusing on what makes us happy or happier, there are two "C's" to consider: connecting and contributing. Connecting with others face to face, eye to eye, increases our empathy and produces serotonin, according to research published in *Child Development*. The added benefit is that the human connection often results in the human touch. It may be a firm handshake, a gentle nudge or a loving pat on the back – all are affirming gestures that connect us physically and emotionally. Contributing to others – giving your time, talent and treasure – is an excellent remedy for the blues. Seek ways to give of yourself for the greater good by contributing to something bigger than yourself, something meaningful to you. Remember, even a simple act of kindness is a great beginning. Multiple studies show that contributing to society – even if it is with one individual at a time – will improve your health, increase your self-worth and enhance your contentment.

Brené Brown, professor and author, says a happier life is ultimately all about mindset: "If you feel more positive, the impact will be profound. What we know matters, but who we are matters more. Those who feel lovable, who love, and who experience belonging simply believe they are worthy of love and belonging." Occasionally the reasons for our own unhappiness are hidden. We may feel down or lethargic but the reason is unclear. In those moments, I have found that if I find a quiet place to have a conversation with myself and explore the reasons for my discontent I can uncover what is bothering me. Asking myself direct questions often brings direct answers. Then I decide what I could do differently, even if it's gradually, to diminish the obstacles to more satisfaction and contentment.

My husband once facilitated this kind of conversation for me, and it is the reason I hang my hat on this approach to happiness self-awareness. We have had a life together filled with contentment and an abundance for which I am tremendously grateful. One day while we were in the car, he asked, "Is there anything in life you would or could change that would make you happier?" I had just asked myself the same question because I had recognized my discontent earlier in the day. Perhaps he had sensed that. I answered him out loud, and suddenly I granted myself the freedom to reprioritize my life and gain his buy-in as well, "Yes, I want to change my daily schedule to include a two-mile walk nearly every day." That was all it took to start a new daily routine that included both exercise and the outdoors as a daily priority.

Identifying what makes you happy can remain a mystery until you concentrate and devote some thought to it. Most people pursue relationships, career advancement or money and material purchases like a new car in the quest for happiness. Try shifting the focus to meaningful self-fulfillment and living your life with purpose. Is your career meaningful work that serves your passion? If not, are you involved in organizations that provide meaning, purpose and an opportunity to support your passion? The way to begin feeling happier is by doing something that helps others, serves a higher purpose and gives a part of yourself for a greater good.

My husband and I went to Africa for our 20th wedding anniversary. For months leading up to the trip, I assured him we would be safe and that every detail had been planned. What I conveniently didn't mention is that we were going on a group tour. Yes, I was gambling that we would enjoy people we had never met – for two weeks (fourteen days and evenings). Our tour included a dinner hosted by a South African couple, friends of our chaperone guide. It was such a unique evening. Being guests in someone's home was an unexpected cultural experience, a wonderful bonus to our vacation. I was intrigued by our hosts and grateful to have the opportunity to understand their country and their community though their eyes. Our hostess was intrigued by the jacket I was wearing that evening. It was my favorite accessory, a long, black sweater with a bit of frilly trim. It was both comfortable and stylish. The perfect travel sweater jacket. It never wrinkled and always looked great. I could roll it up and use it for a pillow, then wear it again and it would still look good. During that trip, the lions, giraffes, zebras and elephants were all amazing. But what I remember so clearly is how good I felt as we pulled out of our host's driveway knowing she had discovered that I had left my jacket for her. It was gratifying because this spontaneous gifting was new to me. I really had no idea it felt that good.

Many people believe success brings happiness and that success is defined as achievement. But if achievement is defined as possessions or social status, you will be perpetually chasing an illusion. I remember commenting to Lowell years ago that perhaps it takes a comfortable financial position to realize that it is not money that brings contentment. In other words, once we achieved financial stability, it became clear that a sense of purpose and an appreciation for the relationships we cherish are the ingredients for true contentment. Research conducted by Ruut Veenhoven, Dutch sociologist, a pioneer and world authority on the scientific study of happiness, revealed that happiness refers to satisfaction with life *as a whole*. It covers past, present and anticipated experiences. It includes the bonds of human connection and feeling that our lives are purposeful.

Part III

Live Well

Chapter 6

Prepare Yourself

"You can't invent events. They just happen.
But you have to be prepared to deal with
them when they happen."
Constance Baker Motley

Move Forward by Letting Go of the Past
"If you have made mistakes, even serious ones,
there is always another chance for you.
What we call failure is not the falling down,
but the staying down."
Mary Pickford

Live for today, plan for tomorrow and learn from the mistakes of yesterday. It may sound easy – and honorable. Learn, change, move forward. It sounds freeing. But for many of us, our mistakes are difficult to process and even more difficult to leave behind. Our guilt and remorse linger. Learn to forgive yourself. Make peace with it. Recognize that you are here today, and you are okay. Your past does not define you or limit you. It allows you to learn and prepares you for the future.

Lydia Fenet, author of the book *The Most Powerful Woman in the Room is You: Command an Audience and Sell Your Way to Success*, reminds us, "There will be rejection and failures along the way, and you may worry those failures will define you. Trust that you will grow stronger with each failure. In time, you will understand why you needed to go through those moments in order to be prepared for even more challenging life experiences." The more time you spend on old and irrelevant issues, the less productive and proactive you are. I, too, have to "process" my mistakes. Sometimes I hear myself saying, "I will be glad when time passes so I can stop beating myself up over this!"

Successful people acknowledge that an essential part of growth is failure. We reflect on our failures to learn from our mistakes, then we move forward. The key is to constantly remind yourself that you have new strength and knowledge from what you have learned. But Barbara Fredrickson, in her book *Positivity*, describes two negative emotions that hold us back from rebounding with greater strength. It is the difference, she says, between inappropriate negativity and appropriate negativity. The negative emotions we experience after we have made a mistake can often be categorized as guilt or shame. Guilt stems from our awareness that we did something wrong. Shame is a bit more debilitating and can be a force much more difficult to contend with, holding us back. Our shame tends to create self-judgment that we are wrong, that we are immoral, that we do not measure up. It can mushroom and cloud our vision; this is referred to as gratuitous negativity. Gratuitous negativity is harmful and unhealthy. It moves our thoughts in a negative direction and multiplies them. It creates a style of thinking called rumination that blows a situation up out of proportion. When we ruminate, our thoughts become like trains, lengthening and picking up speed. We go over our mistakes – or someone else's mistakes – again and again. It distorts our perspective, increases our negative emotions and drags us down. When you sense this behavior taking hold, find a healthy activity that will totally distract you. This helps take your mind in another direction. It can break the cycle of your rumination. Appropriate and necessary negativity grounds us in the reality that we are on a journey of continuous improvement and allows us to move forward and flourish. It does not require us to languish. We recognize that there are clear ways to resolve our mistakes. We make amends, we apologize, we right our wrongs and we find better, more considerate ways to behave in the future. We apply the lessons from our mistakes to guide us in the future.

Optimism: Believe You Can Do It and You Can!

"You gain strength, courage, and confidence by every experience in which you really stop to look fear in the face. You must do the thing which you think you cannot do."
Eleanor Roosevelt

"If you think you can't, you're right. And if you think you can, you're right," said Henry Ford more than one hundred years ago. Why do you stand a better chance of success if you are an optimist? Individuals who are optimistic learn from failure; they analyze their mistakes so they can modify their approach. While a pessimist may sulk after a disappointment or blame someone or something for the outcome, an optimist will find the silver lining, adjust their approach, rework their plan and move forward with momentum.

During the first two years of my college career my major was floriculture, the study of cut plants and indoor flowers. I had chosen that field of study after commenting to my boyfriend, "I have no idea what to major in next year at college." His reply, "Well, you like plants and flowers, right? So major in floriculture, a division of the School of Horticulture in the College of Agriculture." Spoken like a loyal agriculture major himself, he was already enrolled in the Department of Agricultural Economics. I had decided, based on several dynamics of our homelife, that I would skip my junior year of high school and go straight from sophomore to senior year. That would enable me to go off to college in my own fiercely independent way just as quickly as I possibly could. Seeking very little advice and feeling pressure to have a plan in place, there I was, a student on the "ag campus" at The Ohio State University at age 17. As a floriculture major, I began to notice several red flags indicating this was not the perfect fit for me. For instance, during our class daffodil judging contest, all the flowers looked remarkably the same to me. Despite the disconnect with my major, I learned an important lesson as my agronomy final exam approached. I remember saying to a classmate who also lived in my residence hall, "If we dress like farmers, we will think like farmers." We wore our flannel shirts, overalls and ballcaps to our final exam, and yes, we passed. The valuable lesson as a floriculture major for two years was learned that day: If we were positive, optimistic and believed that we could pass, we would. And we did.

Angela Duckworth, author of *Grit: The Power of Passion and Perseverance,* describes this as learned optimism. Optimists are just as likely to encounter a difficult, challenging or negative situation as a pessimist. The difference is their approach. An optimist will search for the cause to a problem. They assume it is temporary and able to be resolved. A pessimist is more likely to assume it is permanent, hopeless, that they are helpless and that there is someone or something to blame.

Studies show optimists tend to earn higher grades, achieve more in their careers, are healthier and ultimately live longer. They are also more satisfied in their marriages. Studies also show that your degree of optimism may reflect your mindset. A person with a fixed mindset interprets the role they can play in the world as limited by their own static intelligence and talent. Individuals with a growth-oriented mindset believe they can continue to learn, improve and achieve. They believe if they try hard enough, anything is possible.

Choosing positive, encouraging language in our self-talk and providing encouragement in our actions and responses as parents, friends, teachers and mentors can increase a growth mindset. This can translate into overcoming adversities and enjoying an optimistic perspective in life. We reinforce in ourselves and others that we can learn to do what we could not do before. It is the difference between effort and natural talent, which is why praise for effort helps develop a positive, growth-oriented mindset, a component of an optimistic outlook that contributes to success. As Duckworth says regarding mindset and optimism, "Language is one way to cultivate hope. But modeling a growth mindset –

demonstrating by our actions that we truly believe people can learn to learn – may be even more important."

Practice optimistic self-talk and modify your perspective so you do not allow setbacks and adversity to discourage you for long. You can change the way you think, feel and, most importantly, act when the going gets tough. Winston Churchill once said, "A pessimist sees the difficulty in every opportunity; an optimist sees the opportunity in every difficulty."

When I accepted a position as a marketing representative (aka sales representative) for Eastman Kodak Company, I requested to work in the government and education markets. Not really understanding why, my gut told me that I would be a good fit in those markets. After nearly instant success during my initial year, my manager shared with me that he and others had chuckled about my request because it had always been a challenging market niche. After several years of success, I was promoted to the government account specialist for the southern United States. In that role, as well, I found myself successful. Then a position became available for a government account specialist for the Southeast region across all product lines for the company. It would mean a huge promotion for me within the company, but I did not apply for the position. The evening before the posting closed, one of the regional managers asked me to apply. The next day I was interviewed and offered the job. I believe, between you and me, it had been created with me in mind. But I had not even considered the opportunity. I lacked confidence in my abilities and lacked optimism for my future advancement.

Optimistic, positive individuals believe in themselves. Even without a specific end goal in mind, they say yes to opportunities that lead to growth and learning and to a culture that encourages mentorship and support. If we have a growth mindset and believe we can improve, we are not fearful or daunted by an acknowledgment that we will need to grow into where we need to be. "Building on your strengths multiplies your efforts," says Valorie Burton. "Excuses allow us to justify our lack of progress. Instead, choose to positively coach yourself." Starting with your speech, eliminate negative phrases such as "I can never learn this" or "I always mess this up." A better way to frame something that has not gone well is to say to yourself, "Next time I am going to try xyz because I think that may work out better than how I handled abc today!" Try to view difficult or tricky experiences as a positive challenge rather than a negative situation. With optimism, we can face life's challenges with agility, ready to create positive change.

Prepare: Make a Plan and Work Your Plan

"Whatever job you are asked to do at whatever level, do a good job because your reputation is your resume."
Madeleine Albright

Planning is the power tool used to achieve everything in life. Once we appreciate the edge that being well-prepared provides, we do not give it up. The key is creating a plan and then working the plan. To plan well, first visualize the desired result, just as I visualized passing an Agronomy final exam. To work a plan, set incremental steppingstone goals that lead to the attainment of the overall goal. Ideas will not become real without an implemented plan. What will look as though it was effortless – whether it is a project, a presentation, or an event – has countless hours of preparation beforehand and behind the scenes. Quickly learn to appreciate the edge that preparation gives you and the euphoric feeling of having not just a job well done, but a job done to the absolute best of your ability.

Preparation reduces stress and increases your self-confidence. The more you prepare, the more relaxed you are. I learned these lessons best while working as a director of catering for Hyatt Hotels. Two weeks before any major convention opening, we held a "pre-con" meeting. This pre-convention meeting was attended by every divisional manager as well as the executive management team. The convention decision-makers, the meeting planner and his/her staff were on site and in attendance. Each divisional manager reviewed how they had prepared for the convention attendees. They reviewed any special requests and any significant details made by the convention meeting planner(s). I always found it fascinating that thousands of convention attendees would descend on our hotel completely absorbed in an industry I had little knowledge of. We hosted the national association of just about everything. It was interesting to contemplate the industry-specific details of these different associations at our pre-con meetings. My favorite pre-con meeting and convention was with Jack Hanna, the legendary zookeeper and director of the Columbus Zoo and Aquarium in Ohio, who was the host for a zoological association. I remember being equally mesmerized by the National Hospital Administrators convention while I walked the exhibit floor and saw the hundreds of vendors whose livelihoods were in industries I did not even know existed. The staff favorite was always the Ohio Funeral Directors Association, which is so amusing because I am now one of *them*. We would walk through their convention hall and remark on how noticeably excited the attendees were about morbid items like caskets and burial vaults. Regardless of the industry or the convention, these pre-convention meetings were critical and a model for successful planning. First, we brought all the crucial members of the team together so that everyone could be in concert with each other for a unified delivery. It allowed the organizers to share their vision for a successful outcome, and it gave everyone the opportunity to articulate how we had prepared for incoming guests. Professionally reciting our plans, department by department, and memorializing them in writing to disseminate at the meeting created structure and accountability. A working plan calls for fluidity and flexibility, but the elements of vision, mission, desired outcome and steps toward achieving the outcome are always critical.

Planning and preparation apply to everything worth doing in life – from projects you want to accomplish by yourself to experiences you want to enjoy with others. When I decided at 55 to go back to school to earn a master's degree, I knew I would need to allocate time strictly for school. I knew it would require perseverance, discipline, sacrifice and a well-planned schedule. At the time, I was working in corporate development for the company that had purchased our funeral homes and cemeteries. One of my responsibilities included representing our company at trade association conventions across the country. In the spring that year, the convention was held in New Orleans – not a sleepy city. Each night, plenty of entertainment stretched into the late hours of the evening. It was customary that when the educational sessions ended and the trade show exhibit floor closed, groups of vendor-partners and colleagues would enjoy lavish dinners together. I enjoyed being included in one such evening, but I also knew I was growing dangerously close to a deadline for a grad school paper that required my full attention. I excused myself as soon as dinner had ended when the fun was just about to begin for most of them. I had to claim the remainder of the evening for myself. Even now, I remember being back in my hotel room and getting so tired as I worked on my paper that I set my alarm for midnight, went to bed at ten o'clock and returned to my paper after a two-hour nap to work another three hours before returning to bed. The payoff is that achieving your goal is worth the planning, the preparation and the sacrifice. We all know the great feeling of accomplishment from having a good plan and the perseverance to see it through.

A variety of examples can illustrate how proper planning creates better outcomes. It is natural to envision positive results, but positive results typically do not occur without positive intentions defined in a plan. For one of my significant "speed limit" birthdays, we hosted a group of family and friends on a destination birthday weekend extravaganza. For each group dinner, I had arranged the seating in advance. To the meeting planners I had hired, it may have seemed silly to plan seating assignments for every dinner meal, but I insisted.

What I knew – and perhaps they may not have realized – was that without seating assignments intentionally ensuring that different family members and friends would mix and mingle, our guests would have gravitated to others they already knew. My plan was successful. Many of our family members and friends commented how much they enjoyed getting to know others in the group whom they had never talked with before.

Preparation – the opposite of "winging it" – is a critical part of every accomplishment. Preparing for meetings and conversations by writing notes is an excellent start. For important opportunities, your advance notes can assist you in covering all the essential elements of a program or project required for its success. Jotting down talking points can help you stay on track. When my husband or I visit our accountant, our attorney or our doctor, we walk in with notes. We have our questions or concerns written down. We have reminders of issues we want to discuss. Walking in prepared allows us to get the most out of the appointment. For difficult conversations, talking points can help you remain objective and on point. You have less of a chance to allow your emotions to hijack a conversation.

Routines, habits and systems bring a degree of predictability that prepares you for whatever lies ahead. Creating routines keeps you on time and on track. The tone of your day is set by how you start your day. Routines bring calmness. There is a sense of composure from knowing what you expect to come next. Plans can change, but your preparedness will keep you agile. It will position you to handle challenges as they arise.

Going back to school to earn my master's degree, I knew I would need to make a plan, work the plan and work as hard as I could for a positive outcome. The process started successfully because of that knowledge. Much of working that plan came from the preparation it took to simply get accepted. The next step was "clearing the deck" of other commitments and distractions. The preparation for acceptance and the fear of not being accepted were both intense. I knew I needed to be able to say I gave it my best. I prepared as much as I could to ensure I was chosen for the program. You cannot bypass hard work and effort. It was months before I received my acceptance letter, a joyous moment. I have found that what is gratifying is not always instantaneous and the wait increases the appreciation.

Review various aspects of your life; are you preparing yourself financially, physically, emotionally and professionally? Financial preparation means that you are systematically saving money and living within your means. Physical preparation is how well you take care of your body with good eating habits, exercise and good sleeping routines. Your emotional preparation involves positive relationships with your spouse, partner, family and close friends. It means loving yourself and communicating effectively with those you care about. Additionally, it includes learning, cultivating mentors and networking.

"The difference between people who achieve their goals and people who don't is their ability to dust themselves off and wear their dirty outfit proudly," says author Emily Ley. The more you work your plan, even when (not if) you mess up, the sooner you will know when and how to alter your plan to make it work out in the end. It is okay to fall and get dirty along the way.

Invest in Your Personal and Professional Growth

"The ability to learn is the most important quality a leader can have."
Sheryl Sandberg

In life, just as in business, we have a responsibility for our own discipline and personal growth. Great leaders are committed to ongoing learning. They stay ahead in a competitive environment. They stay abreast of current issues in their field. They gain knowledge about current events and political affairs and can easily participate in and contribute to any casual or professional conversation. It is important to plan and implement opportunities to strengthen professional growth by managing your own personal training program. What you are going to be tomorrow, you are becoming today.

Harvard Business Review's *Management Tips* suggests ways to "stay sharp" as you take responsibility for your growth: Meet with two coworkers each month. Discuss the industry you are in and where it is headed. Plan one major challenge each quarter that will provide a new learning experience. If your work is not giving you exciting challenges, seek out other opportunities, such as volunteering for a nonprofit, attending a conference or taking a class. Another way to stay sharp is by giving yourself honest performance reviews, then reflecting on your growth. Ask for peer feedback. Be honest with yourself about your strengths and weaknesses and what you should focus on in the coming year to improve. Occasionally people have shared with me their own deficiencies and most of the time it concerned a job skill they were lacking. A helpful way to respond is, "So I 'did this' and now I am competent in that area."

When our animal shelter CEO asked me to chair its first-ever capital campaign, I was not even a board member. I had no knowledge of the inner workings of the animal shelter nor did I really know a great deal about animal welfare. In fact, I knew nothing about animal care except from my own experience with our adopted cats. I was a believer in rescuing and not purchasing. I know there is a place in this world for beautiful purebreds purchased by loving pet parents. Most breeders are not puppy mills, and I believe most educated, caring pet parents would not purchase from puppy mills. Nonetheless, our hearts are with rescued animals. The day I met with the shelter CEO, I was at a crossroads or perhaps at the end of the road with my career in funeral service. We had sold our family businesses, fourteen funeral homes and cemeteries. I had continued my employment with the firm that purchased us for a number of years following the sale and I had transitioned from a regional management position to a role in corporate development. But the writing was on the wall regarding the company's acquisition future, so I made the decision to retire. During the subsequent five years, I used my lighter schedule to accomplish a few goals: earning my master's degree and taking on the role of capital campaign chair to renovate and expand our local animal shelter. I made these decisions because I was offered an opportunity to learn something new. I was offered an opportunity to work side-by-side with a professional development consultant along with the shelter CEO. I was intrigued. I had the opportunity to invest in my own professional development and accept a $3.6 million fundraising challenge.

Extending yourself beyond your comfort

zone, trying new things, overcoming fear, improving personal habits and creating uplifting surroundings can all be a result of your own investment in yourself. Embracing technology leads to empowering yourself. Taking the time and putting forth the effort to harness the tools you have at your fingertips will lead to greater satisfaction and a sense of accomplishment. Feeling deficient with popular electronic tools such as an iPhone and an iPad, popular apps and common software products can be overcome with local college classes, one-on-one help from a friend or colleague or with one of my favorite methods – YouTube instructional videos. I think there is a teaching video on nearly every imaginable subject. I believe we can always continue to learn.

It's Jack Nicklaus Time!

"I am not a has-been. I am a will be."
Lauren Bacall

My husband leaned over to me and said, "It's Jack Nicklaus time!" Months before, he had watched a television interview with Jack Nicklaus. The television announcer asked him how he held up against the pressure – knowing there were millions of television viewers and thousands of spectators gathered around to watch him sink or not sink a final putt for the win. Jack Nicklaus responded,

"Are you kidding? It's what I live for!"

Now, minutes before a family member takes the stage or takes the floor, we turn to each other and repeat our familiar mantra. Take the stage and enjoy your moment. Know that you can make your putt whether it is presenting a business proposal, chairing a meeting, teaching a class or giving a speech. Believing in yourself is the key, as well as knowing that you are prepared and ready to deliver.

For public speaking success, again, preparation is the key. Practicing a speech or presentation is critical. When I prepare for a speech, I perform it a minimum of ten times. Those can be long hours of preparation if a presentation is lengthy. But it is worth every minute. I would rather blunder while knowing I was as prepared as possible, than blunder and know I could have avoided it with proper preparation. Good preparation also allows you to connect with your audience more effectively because you are embracing them with your eye contact, smile and hand gestures, not looking at, or worse yet, reading your notes. If that is too nerve-racking for you, memorize your opening remark and your closing remark. By memorizing your opening line, you ensure that you are looking out into your audience and engaging with them. Showing your enthusiasm is critical. Speaking on a subject that you know inside and out, and that you are passionate about, creates energy inside of you that can be shared with your audience naturally.

Opening a presentation with a story is an effective way to begin because you know the story. You do not have to memorize a story if it is yours. And if it is possible, save a bit of the story for your close, especially if it is unexpected. Tying together your presentation with a story at the beginning and then finishing with the "real ending" to the story provides bookends around your presentation that creates a positive audience response. You can also engage your audience during your speech by asking them a question. This audience engagement creates energy in the room and energizes you. It makes them feel a part of your presentation; you are now talking with them, not at them.

People gravitate to charismatic and authentic leaders, colleagues and friends. This gravitational force applies to both professional and personal relationships. Authenticity is created when others sense we are showing them our true selves, when we show others our hearts. That is why rehearsing, role-playing and preparing for presentations creates a sense of spontaneity. It allows us to be relaxed. In his book *Trust Me: Four Steps to Authenticity and Charisma,* Nick Morgan states that being open and connected creates a relationship and demonstrates charisma. Then, being passionate and being a good listener helps convey our authenticity. Our presence, both verbally and nonverbally, communicates that we are open to sharing with our audience. Our audience must know that we are engaged with them. Authenticity, as described by author Brené Brown, is the daily practice of letting go of who we think we are supposed to be and embracing who we really are. In this case, it means allowing others to sense who we really are. It means cultivating the courage to be imperfect and exercising compassion from the knowledge that we are all made of strengths and struggles. She goes on to say that when we mindfully practice authenticity during our most soul-searching struggles, we invite grace, joy and gratitude into our lives. These qualities are appreciated by our audience.

According to author Lydia Fenet, a powerful woman is authentic in the way she sells herself and her vision to other people. She is unafraid to present who she is and what she has accomplished. She knows that people will believe in her when she believes in what she is presenting and when she uses her personality to engage people. I have experienced this first-hand with three capital campaign initiatives that I have chaired. In each capital campaign, I have envisioned the result, felt passionately about the need and in turn engaged others to participate with me.

Preparation to be your own "Jack Nicklaus" as a presenter also requires several basics. First, get a good night's sleep. Second, if you are preparing for a presentation or an important meeting, select your wardrobe the evening before. Feeling confident is often boosted by the outfit you choose. I would not leave that to chance the next morning. If a presentation or meeting is out of town, try on clothing, shoes and accessories before leaving home. I have often realized that my vision of what I should wear looked entirely different in real life once I put it on. Taking the time to prepare has paid off; I have never regretted that investment of time and effort. Lastly, your presentation should always allow time to test the equipment and perform a sound-and-video check.

Break the People-Pleasing Habit

*"You can't please everyone, and you
can't make everyone like you."*
Katie Couric

My sister Ann wrote to my mother once, "I wish Nancy didn't feel it was so necessary to have the approval of others." She was right. It was a burden and a curse that often left me feeling defensive. Author John Ortberg's term "approval addiction" can explain why we often respond so strongly and negatively to criticism: "We live in bondage to what others think of us." So, when we disappoint someone or are criticized by others, we do not respond with our best selves. I realized later in life that I cannot have a free and gracious life if I am simultaneously bothered by someone who apparently for no reason has chosen to disapprove of me.

The flip side, of course, is not caring at all what others think. This attitude may shield us from being hurt, but it also means we aren't connecting with others. "Courage is telling our story, not being immune to criticism," according to author Brené Brown. "Staying vulnerable is a risk we have to take if we want to experience connection."

Many women, including me, have grappled with the belief that we must be both tough and tender – the yin and yang of our professional demeanor. We want to be liked. We want to be perceived as compassionate and empathetic. Certainly, as a funeral director this was a job requirement, and I was never sure whether I measured up. But we must also make tough decisions if we are in a management position or as a self-employed business owner. In Sheryl Sandberg's book *Lean In: Women, Work, and the Will to Lead*, she states that when girls try to lead, they are often labeled as bossy. Boys are seldom called bossy because when they take the lead it does not surprise or offend others. Social cues defining appropriate behavior have in turn silenced some women. Sandberg goes on to write, "Professional ambition is expected of men but is optional – or worse, sometimes even a negative – for women. Aggressive and hard-charging women violate unwritten rules about acceptable social conduct." Her research showed that success and likeability are positively correlated for men and negatively correlated for women. Put another way, our gender expectation for men is that they are driven, aggressive, assertive and decisive. Women are expected to be nurturing, sensitive and communal. So, when life demands that we behave in ways more often attributed to our expectations of men, we are less likely to be embraced. It is why I have often said, "Lowell can be very decisive and people applaud him as a man who knows what he wants. Then I do the same thing and people call me a name." Our forcefulness deviates from expected behavior. The results can shake our confidence. Women are less likely to "go out on that limb" because of the repercussions they have experienced in the past. Author Ken Auletta refers to our self-doubt as a form of self-defense. To protect ourselves from being disliked, we question our abilities and downplay our achievements.

Occasionally our Jack Nicklaus moments demand a combination of our authenticity with necessary, tough decision-making. Our communication may be best received by others if it is "delicately honest communication not brutally honest communication," in Sandberg's words. If we understand that our point of view is our truth, but someone else's point of view is their truth, we will be better listeners, better communicators, better leaders. Of course, in these highly charged and politically polarized times, taking this stance can be challenging.

Self-esteem and self-worth are largely wrapped up in what we feel is the appraisal of our worth by others. As human nature predicts, other people will always evaluate our actions and judge our appearance. If this unsolicited feedback is negative, we allow the criticism to negatively affect us. This makes supporting and connecting with each other all the more important. We can support each other by affirming someone, advocating for someone or promoting someone in the eyes of another, especially if their strength catches others off guard. Connect the unconnected. As Madeleine Albright once said, "There's a special place in hell for women who don't help other women."

Remain true to yourself, not true to what you believe others want you to be. Cherish real friends, those who lift you up rather than tear you down. Learn to be yourself and love yourself. As Margaret Thatcher warned, "If you set out to be liked, you would be prepared to compromise on anything at any time, and you would achieve nothing." This realization can be perpetually challenging.

Follow Up and Follow Through

"You have to have confidence in your ability,
and then be tough enough to follow through."
Rosalynn Carter

We earn the reputation of being dependable from our dedication to follow-up and follow-through. I have often walked out of a meeting wondering whether I would receive what was promised. In the heat of the moment, empty promises can be made. "I will email you that information as soon as I am back in my office." Then you notice days later that the email never arrived. We declare our credibility by doing what we promise and doing it on time.

When Lowell and I finish a speaking engagement, we are often asked for a copy of our book(s). If we have run out of books on location or if we had not thought to bring some along, I am often actually glad that we have none on hand. I could tell the requester to order the book(s) on Amazon. But I see this situation as an opportunity to demonstrate follow up. We always offer to mail a copy. I know that if I follow up and complete the request by mailing a personalized copy of our book addressed and autographed, I am reinforcing my credibility with them by my follow-through. I can just hear their response in my mind: "Wow ... they really did it. They actually followed through."

Be Resilient

> *"You will encounter many defeats,*
> *but you must not be defeated."*
> Maya Angelou

Our lives are plagued with distraction and stress, so it is critical that we find tools to overcome adversity and build resiliency. As author Brené Brown shares, "Find the things we do, the things we have, and the practice that gives us the bounce." Learn to ride the crest of the unexpected wave with composure and confidence. Knowing that you will face stumbling blocks along your journey in life requires that you build a reservoir, a reserve of inner strength. Think of it as your safety net.

One evening Lowell and I were in our family room/kitchen area. I was making us a bite to eat while he searched the television channels for something to snag his interest during the few moments before dinner was ready. He landed on a television broadcast of Les Brown, the motivational speaker. "The Best Revenge is Massive Success!" he bellowed. Revenge seems like such a negative word, but in the context of his presentation, he was conveying the idea that we must channel the negative noise we all hear into a laser focus on accomplishing our goals. As soon as someone or something negative makes me feel bad, I think of Les Brown speaking to us in our home that evening. I channel my energy toward continuing my quest. Be like ducks. Let the negativity roll off your back like water, and do not let others rain on your parade. Your self-worth is not in the hands of others. Remind yourself of your values and goals and do not depend on anyone else to validate them. Everyone's perspective is based on their own life experiences. Do not allow someone else's judgment of your life to be your interpretation. Weed out counterproductive thoughts from the inside and the outside.

We have all heard stories of those who have gone from rags to riches. They gambled – sometimes winning it all and sometimes losing it all. I am guessing they always had a high reserve of resiliency. They could face, thrive and grow in the face of seemingly insurmountable adversity and unthinkable challenges. According to author Brené Brown, there are five common factors in building resiliency. These include being resourceful and a good problem solver, asking for assistance and believing in your own ability to cope. Individuals with resiliency have strong social support; they are connected with others, such as family and friends.

Like a hiker who has the necessary gear to face unexpected terrain along a path, you must have the necessary gear inside you to face future obstacles. And there will be obstacles. But you can be prepared to navigate your path and overcome those obstacles. Your path will rarely be a straight and narrow one. Twists, turns, curves and forks in the road will require decisions and will require plans. Be clear about your own purpose. Remember your individual strengths. Think about the vision you have for yourself in the future. Be excited, enthusiastic and positive about how much stronger and better prepared you will be because of each obstacle. Then move forward.

Preparation, optimism, organization and flexible, positive attitudes aid our resilience. We can prepare ourselves to handle the unexpected. It is our own support system, both internal and external, that enables us to be our best when a crisis occurs or an unexpected challenge presents itself. Positive relationships strengthen our resistance. Nurturing relationships are critical. When the going gets tough, having people in our lives who will listen and offer words of encouragement is critical. We are strengthened by compassionate and empathetic connections. Our achievements are more meaningful because they are shared with others. Conquering situations in our lives, when strength and resilience are required, are aided by those who help, encourage and support us.

Read
"Until I feared I would lose it, I never loved to read.
One does not love breathing."
Harper Lee

Reading is the single common denominator of most successful people. Successful people and great leaders are curious about ideas and the world around them. They crave knowledge. They realize knowledge is critical in decision making. If you recognize that knowledge in a particular area would be helpful in achieving a goal, and you are weak in that area, remember, there is a book written on every subject in the world. Reading books or listening to relevant audio programs is a part of becoming the best version of yourself. Understand and embrace the idea that being active and pursuing your goals includes sitting still and reading.

One year my husband and I remodeled the study that housed most of our books. It was a moment to purge many of the books we had accumulated. I also made the decision to work from home and decided to create my home office, "Nancy's Nest," in what was then our bonus room above the garage. I brought my books up to my nest from the study, sorted through them and discovered that I had never actually read some of them. This was an authenticity gut check for me. Who was I trying to impress? Immediately I vowed that only books I had read and were treasured would go on my new office bookshelves. I then created my reading list – a manageable stack of books. The next addition to my office was a reading chair. My office move reminded me of my intention to read more. I had been too busy doing urgent things instead of doing important things. I had not invested in myself by reading. I vowed to allow myself time to read and to retreat to "Nancy's Nest" often. Warren Buffett concurs. He gravitates to the quietude of his hometown, Omaha, Nebraska, where his daily life centers on reading and gestation. He fondly shares, "Inactivity can be very intelligent behavior."

Know Your One Thing

"Far away there in the sunshine are my
highest aspirations. I may not reach them,
but I can look up and see their beauty,
believe in them, and try to follow
where they lead."
Louisa May Alcott

In the movie *City Slickers*, Curly (played by Jack Palance) says, "You know what the secret to life is? ... one thing, just one thing."

Although most of us would immediately know that our one thing is our spouse, our family, our health and our career, in Gary Keller and Jay Papasan's book *The One Thing: The Surprisingly Simple Truth Behind Extraordinary Results,* they focus on ways to bring more clarity and more positivity to all these areas of our life – family, work and self. "Extraordinary results are directly determined by how narrow you can make your focus." According to Keller and Papasan, "Success is built sequentially. It's one thing at a time." To be as successful as possible, we cannot focus on everything equally. We must sort through the urgent and determine what is important. We must be able to narrow our focus to the one thing that matters most and prioritize our time around it. "Choose what matters most and give it all the time it demands," say Keller and Papasan.

Keller and Papasan focus on "the one thing that you can do such that by doing it everything else will be easier or unnecessary." They apply this question to all facets of life. For instance, they encourage us to ask what the one thing is we can do for our health, for our personal life and for our key relationships. But they also encourage us to ask a focusing question; a question that very specifically answers what the one thing is that we want to accomplish. Our one thing becomes our purpose. I have found that the first step toward prioritizing my life and being laser-focused on a goal, is to memorialize it on paper.

I tried to commit to "one thing" by writing it down. But instead it became a list of my "one things" plural. The good news is that when we commit our goals to paper, we are more apt to act on them. But writing down only one thing was impossible for me. I needed to evaluate options. Different goals appealed to me. It was difficult to define my life and my future with a single purpose. It was as though my one thing needed to bubble up from an assortment of goals and interests. The list required hours of thought and reflection. Many ideas took years to percolate to the top. Others, admittedly, are still waiting their turn.

Determining how we choose to occupy the world depends on what excites us. For example, one person may want to devote their life to education and another to music. By giving thought to and memorializing in writing what we want to accomplish in life, we increase our conviction, and that conviction creates clarity. Knowing what we are committed to allows us to finish this sentence: "I want to be the best I can possibly be at ..." But choosing our one thing does not mean allowing one aspect of our life to dominate the others. It means visualizing a process, prioritizing and taking incremental steps toward a goal so we will achieve it in the future. We must recognize that our priorities will vary at different times in our life, priorities such as career/work, spouse/family, civic contributions, self-improvement (hobbies, wellness) and social engagement (investing in the friendships we treasure). This is why we must make a list, we must memorialize our goals. In addition, write down the strengths that will help you achieve those "one things." Our accomplishments are often related to our innate abilities. Whether it is accuracy, organization, creativity, administrative detail or managing difficult people, being cognizant of your strengths can be a source of encouragement. Your one thing can be a personal goal to try something new. It can be learning a new skill or a new subject. It can be focused on health and self-improvement or it can be very specific to your career.

Choosing your one thing includes long-term dreams but also shorter, one- to two-year goals. And it will always include focus, discipline and hard work. Author Lydia Fenet shares, "Find something you love, something that you are good at doing, and hone your craft with years of practice until you are the best in your field." This process requires "putting in the time." You will gain self-respect as well as respect from your peers and those you admire with the sweat equity of working hard to advance in your field and achieve your personal goals.

Depending on where you are at this moment in life, commemorating your one thing may be difficult. Identifying an "ultimate purpose" is not always easy. Writing down what you find meaningful is an effective exercise to identify your one thing. It could be something creative or contemplative. It could be related to children, the elderly, animal welfare or the arts. It may not have anything to do with your career. You can cultivate your gifts and share them with the world in many ways and at different moments in your life, but you will never recognize that opportunity until you identify where your passion lies. Theologian Howard Thurman said, "Don't ask what the world needs. Ask what makes you come alive and go do it. Because what the world needs is people who have come alive."

Focus on the Important Things and Not the Urgent Things

"Power is the ability to get things done."
Rosabeth Moss Kanter

"I'm too busy doing the urgent things to do the important things." Stephen Covey points out this commonly heard refrain in his book, *The 7 Habits of Highly Effective People: Powerful Lessons in Personal Change.* Keller and Papasan refer to surfing through the urgent to determine the important. Many things are not urgent; in fact, they may not even be important, but they serve as distractors and they steal hours away from us. To maximize our days, we must articulate "what is the best use of my time?" on an ongoing basis. If we allow distractions such as social media to interfere in achieving our goals, we must discipline ourselves with limitations. If you find you are tackling tasks that someone else in your organization could accomplish just as easily, then delegate.

Prioritize scheduling based on what you need to accomplish, short term and long term. "Urgent" means life or death. Everything else falls into priorities. Important things we want to accomplish often require larger blocks of time, and mundane tasks can rob us of these blocks of time before we know it. I plan blocks of time – "Nancy Time" – in advance that allow me to focus on accomplishing a specific goal. Typically, I retreat to my nest. Whether I am reading a book, writing a magazine article, thinking through a project or working through the logistics of an event, I prioritize that block of time. When I am planning my week, I calendar those blocks. Setting aside time in advance to do what is important allows me to resist the temptation of interference and distraction.

Creating systems is critical, and time management ranks right at the top. Creating structure in your life and in your organization will help you handle the unexpected with composure while you are working toward larger, more important goals, especially if those goals come with deadlines. Be a leader who creates and respects systems, particularly time management, because good systems and structure are required to consistently achieve excellent results.

Write it Down

"Write what should not be forgotten."
Isabel Allende

Journaling or memorializing your thoughts, plans and your "one thing" in writing can give you a clarity that cannot be created in any other way. Writing about what you hope to accomplish makes your goals clearer. Writing about what is bothering you creates a way to vent and lessens the overwhelming sense of the problem. Writing allows you to tune out the world and focus on a specific issue or quest.

Writing acknowledges. Writing validates. Writing can be therapeutic. Writing can be cathartic. That is why journaling can help a person cope with a traumatic experience, such as losing a loved one. It is a tool for increasing our self-awareness. It helps us process events and helps us realize fully "what we are feeling." When we have a need for analytical thinking, focusing our attention through writing can help us reflect, problem-solve and reprioritize.

Many years ago, I decided to make some lists because it seemed the best way to reflect on my priorities in many different areas of my life. My lists ranged from experiences to relationships to goals. They included the best experiences in my life, favorite places, those I would like to return to, my biggest indulgences, the most fascinating things I have seen, what I am most thankful for, areas of interest that I wanted to study and who I consider my lifelong friends. Included was the list of all the "one things" I wanted to accomplish in the future.

And finally, I made a list of all the people to whom I wanted to show the depth of my appreciation. That list led me to reach out to each of those individuals with a personal letter of thanks and to express my regret for not having shown the true depth of my gratitude. Had I not written this list of individuals, that clarity may not have come.

Writing can change our perspective. It can make us feel like an outsider looking in. We look at ourselves more objectively. I knew that those on my acknowledgment list were there for a reason. One was a girlfriend who had visited her winter home in Florida. I canceled our get-together at the last minute because of a pressing situation at the funeral home. I felt badly that I had allowed either my poor planning or a lack of prioritizing to interfere with our plans to see each other, and I knew I had hurt her feelings. I had essentially communicated that something was more important than our time together. I did not display the appreciation for our relationship that she deserved. Sadly, I cannot even remember what that day's crisis was at the funeral home, which is even more telling. Reaching out to those on my list was cleansing. I could not right my wrongs, but I could apologize and show my appreciation for all they had done and had given me.

Writing creates self-awareness. It forces us to slow down and reflect. Writing allows us to evaluate and reevaluate the pros and cons of a situation or a plan we are creating. As author Valorie Burton shares, "Success is intentional, and writing is a powerful way to be intentional. It is a form of self-coaching." Author Brené Brown suggests writing a list called "Ingredients for Joy and Meaning." This is a list of specific conditions that are in place when everything feels good in your life. What are your most rewarding experiences? Who do you treasure most in your life? Which goals are most important to you right now? What do you want to do differently in your life starting right now? Writing can be your tool for self-exploration and for self-reflection. It can help us deliberate about what is valuable and precious in our lives.

Monotask, not Multitask

"Multitasking is like constantly pulling up a plant.
This kind of constant shifting of your attention means
that new ideas and concepts have no chance
to take root and flourish."
Barbara Oakley

Compelling research by the American Psychological Association reveals that what you think is efficient multitasking is actually an ineffective means of accomplishing tasks. According to studies, as you switch from one task to another, the transition is not a smooth one. There is a lag time while your brain shifts attention from one task to another. The shift may feel seamless, but it takes time. Research has shown that when a person is multitasking, it takes as much as 40 percent more time to complete the tasks compared to focusing on one task at a time – and the percentage is even higher for complex tasks.

"What looks like multitasking is really switching back and forth between multiple tasks, which reduces productivity and increases mistakes by up to 50 percent," according to author Susan Cain. Businesswoman and television personality Karen Finerman adds, "When you multitask, you believe you're being exceptionally productive, but really, you're fooling yourself. Each time you switch tasks, you have to backtrack a little and remind yourself where you are in the process and what is next. Invariably, you are spending more time on each task." You are also likely to be enjoying the tasks less. By being less engaged you are less fulfilled. To prove this to yourself – practice. Discipline yourself by choosing a task and committing to the completion of the task without interruption. If you are talking on the phone with a friend, do not check emails; if you are on a conference call, do not text; if you are brushing your teeth, do not try to make the bed. If you are tackling a lengthy project, reward yourself by planning breaks in advance at certain milestones. I believe you will find this level of focus and engagement more satisfying. This also applies when interacting with other people in person. In this common situation, multitasking becomes a synonym for being rude. When you are with others – guests, colleagues, friends or family – be sure to put your phone away. Be purposeful about "being in the moment" when you have set aside time to be with others.

Take Charge of Your Finances and Your Financial Freedom

"Change your life today. Don't gamble on the future, act now, without delay."
Simone de Beauvoir

"Educating yourself about money," according to author Lydia Fenet, "means how to use it, how to spend it, how to make it, how to save it, how to make more of it – it is one of the most important things you can do in your life." You are responsible for understanding where your money comes from and where it goes. You are responsible for your financial security. Understanding what it means to be in good financial standing is essential to financial freedom, which in turn is critical for contentment and fulfillment in life. Financial wellness is an incredible gift you give yourself. Knowledge about money is powerful in life because it provides freedom and independence.

My wake-up call for financial wellness came

while I was living in Lexington, Kentucky. One Saturday morning, the day after payday, I sat in my apartment and realized I had more monthly bills than I had monthly income. Suddenly the matching bathroom towels no longer seemed that important. I was nervous. I felt the stress and pressure of my poor financial decisions. I put myself on a strict budget and decided that I had to work my way out of debt and begin living within my means. I curtailed extravagances like going out for dinner after work and going on shopping sprees. It was a difficult path forward, but I managed, one minimum credit card payment at a time. I was thankful I had the sense at age 25 not to ruin my credit. Fast forward, at 27 I bought my first condominium and at 29 I bought my first home and began renting my condominium to offset the mortgage. I remember comments made by my mortgage broker, who subsequently became a neighbor and a dear friend. She still laughs at how I explained my past financial history in such detail during my loan application and approval process. I apparently was excited to share my new financial wisdom.

There are basic rules regarding financial accountability: Rule #1 – Don't enter the new year with a bloated credit card. The holidays are notorious for budget-blowing. Remember to stay within a predetermined holiday budget. Shop all year round, especially during sales, keeping your eyes open for the perfect gifts for those on your holiday gift-giving list. This strategy will minimize out-of-control spending, especially on last-minute gifts.

Rule #2 – Don't borrow from family and friends. And do not lend money to family and friends. Turning your relationships into financial affairs, in most cases, does not end well. Lowell often says, "If you loan a friend or family member money, that implies you are expecting them to pay you back. Most of the time they will not and most of the time it results in losing a friend. Instead, give them a monetary gift or do not, but never consider it a loan."

Rule #3 – Be cognizant of your overconsumption. Overconsuming as I did with my matching bath towels is all too common. We want more and we want it faster, better, bigger and now. Another wake-up call came in the course of near isolation for months during the COVID-19 pandemic. For nearly eight weeks, I wore a fraction of my clothes and had ample opportunity to clean out every drawer and closet in the house. I already had very little clutter, but I was motivated to lessen my load even further. Memes and videos spread across social media as quickly as the virus spread, describing how our dress code changed to strictly activewear and how our eating habits deteriorated along with our hygiene. I realized I possessed much more than I needed and I realized some of my spending habits were a result of entertaining myself instead of focusing on a project that could be meaningful and bring real contentment.

Rule #4 – Learn to negotiate and always seek three bids on any contracted work. I learned a difficult lesson years ago when my husband said, "Some of our friends will be the highest priced." Early in our relationship he insisted that we should always get three bids on any home-improvement project or repair. He was right. I was stunned. Unless it is a loyal and trusted contractor, and we now gratefully have many, always get three bids, it will save you money.

Rule #5 – Systematically save. Investing money over time is the only way to gain financial freedom. As author Robert Kiyosaki says in *Rich Dad Poor Dad: What the Rich Teach Their Kids About Money – That the Poor and Middle Class Do Not!*, "The secret to wealth is time." This is the first of several investment fundamentals. When I met Lowell, I had been systematically saving money and I owned my own home. Those are two important investment principles critical for financial freedom. Although we live in a country where owning your own home is seemingly becoming less desirable, home ownership remains one of the best opportunities to gain financial independence because you build equity. Lowell and I have bought homes at good prices, then have sold them at an increased value. During home ownership, the monthly mortgage payments pay down principal. It is like a savings plan and an equity investment all in one. By paying down the principal of your home, once it is sold you recoup the principal and receive the equity gain. It is basic and it is very important.

In addition to the rules of financial account-ability, I learned critical investment fundamentals. When we sold our family businesses, Lowell began to read as many books on investments as he could. He highlighted and underlined important para-graphs and shared them with me. He feels strong-ly, as I do, that every woman should understand how to invest money wisely. Several of the books were so compelling that he asked all of us in our family to read them. The lessons I learned from him have been documented in dozens of books and can be summarized in this way: 1) Invest your money with a low-cost brokerage firm like Vanguard. 2) Your investment strategy should include a diver-sified portfolio with two classifications: Equities and Short-Intermediate Bonds. The split should be based on how risk averse you feel, but generally it falls in the neighborhood of a 60-40 split, with 60 percent in equities. 3) The equity investment most recommended is the S&P 500 Index Fund. It has proven over a rolling five-year benchmark, ten-year benchmark and twenty-year benchmark to outper-form 90 percent of the other equity investments in the marketplace.

Once you invest your money, do not touch it. "Stay the course," as Jack Bogle, founder of Vanguard, would say. I also learned from Lowell that you must be able to "follow the money" in your investment accounts. At the end of the year, you must be able to determine how much your money has earned. Do not rely on anyone to provide you with a percentage. As an example, say you invest $1,000. At the end of the year your investment account now has a balance of $1,100, proving that you earned a 10 percent return. Often, individuals cannot tell how much their investments have earned because they have diligently deposited money into their account throughout the year or have withdrawn funds. Although systematically saving money is critical, at the end of the year, such investors cannot determine exactly how much was earned. They need a system that allows them to easily follow their money.

In order to systematically save, yet still be able to know how much return you have earned on your investment, create two investment accounts (note: in a brokerage firm such as Vanguard, having multiple accounts does not cost more). In one account invest a portion of your money as an even lump sum. If you have $10,000, invest $6,000 in the S&P 500 Index Fund. Then invest the remaining $4,000 in a Bond Index Fund, a 60-40 split or a different ratio you prefer. Then open a second account and invest a nominal amount of money. Use this second account for the money you systematically save throughout the year. Invest this account using the same investment ratio, a 60-40 split of equities and bonds or whatever ratio you chose in the first account. At the end of the year, you will know exactly how much money you have earned based on the results of the first account. At the end of the year, consider moving some of the funds from your second account into your first account. But, be sure to do it so that you again have an even amount in each of your investments at the first of the year so that you can more easily track your earnings. Follow the money!

Nurture Your "Learner Instinct" with Travel

*"One of the secrets to staying young
is to always do things you don't
know how to do, to keep learning."*
Ruth Reichl

Positivity comes in many forms. Most people use the word "happy" to describe their positive feelings. But Barbara Fredrickson, author of *Positivity*, describes a more specific palette of positive emotions. She categorizes our positive and happy emotions into ten specific subtleties: gratitude, serenity, hope, pride, amusement, inspiration, awe, love, joy and interest.

This explains why nurturing your learner instinct can create excitement and happiness. Examining what triggers our unique interests uncovers why we are excited to conquer new challenges and why we are pulled toward new skills to learn and new places to explore. When we are interested in experiencing or learning about something new, we feel open and alive.

Fascination with human behavior makes traveling an ideal way to fulfill a learner spirit. It provides opportunities to experience a variety of cultures and observe different lifestyles. It is summed up by my favorite quote: "Travel is the only thing we buy that makes us richer" (Anonymous). Sheryl Sandberg states that the desire to learn is the most important quality a leader can possess. Traveling inspires us to learn. It lures us with insightful and comparative observations about our world and allows us to lose ourselves in the intriguing unknown. Like Maslow's hierarchy of human needs, travel can be depicted in similar hierarchical tiers. At the foundation is the most basic motivational need, the human desire to explore. Once the most basic level is fulfilled, we continue to reach for the next levels, including enlightenment and self-awareness.

Travel helps us gain an appreciation for different customs around the world. It broadens our awareness and introduces us to diversity in people. It educates us. It can transform us into more empathetic and more compassionate human beings. It can help remove the biases, prejudices and stereotypes we have developed through the narrow lens of our limited experience. It can improve our tolerance and acceptance.

Several years ago, I planned a trip to Iceland. I had no idea what to expect from Icelanders or from the country itself. I had learned it was a country with enticing outdoor adventures. After an afternoon of touring and hiking, we ended our day at the world-famous Reynisfjara shore, near the village Vik in Myrdalur on Iceland's south coast. It is widely regarded as the most impressive black-sand beach in Iceland. The area features amazing cliffs with dramatic basalt columns in spectacular shapes called Reynisdrangar. The Reynisfjara shore has rich birdlife, including Puffins, Fulmars and Guillemots, but we saw very little wildlife that day because the black beaches were shadowed by gray skies and thick mists of rain matched by waves that were especially intense. Our guide, on the other hand, was relaxed and welcoming. He shared his thoughts on all things Iceland. He described the healthy ways he and his fellow Icelanders live. He told us how they eat organic foods, protect and enjoy nature and power their country with clean hydropower. He reminded us that Iceland is considered the safest place in the world and that kindness and nonviolence are integral parts of Icelandic culture. He encouraged us to notice that there were very few signs listing rules and regulations. Even in relationships, regulations seem unnecessary. In fact, he shared that most marriages in Iceland are not a legal relationship as they are in the United States. There is no need for such a binding arrangement. He had a deep sense of loyalty to his country and its culture. I left feeling an appreciation for Iceland that was completely unexpected and nurtured by the open dialogue we shared with our guide. I no longer saw Iceland from my perspective. I now saw it through his eyes.

Traveling can make us less fearful. It can make us more engaged with the world. It can make us wiser. Travel broadens our perspective. As well-known travel expert and author Rick Steves shared, "The flip side of fear is understanding. Your world views change when you meet others whose world view is different than yours. Travel changes your ethnocentrisms."

Travel can be great for self-discovery, for appreciating nature and the aesthetic beauty of the world. Travel connects us to people, places and experiences that enrich and expand us. Ultimately at the top of the hierarchy of human needs, travel influences us and affects us. We become better human beings for having traveled.

Focus on *Personal* Measures of Success

"As life goes on it becomes tiring to keep up the
character you invented for yourself,
and so you relapse into individuality
and become more like yourself every day.
This is sometimes disconcerting for
those around you, but a great
relief to the person concerned."
Agatha Christie

Mary McLeod Bethune, founder of a college now known as Bethune-Cookman University, left us words of wisdom that inspire and encourage us all. Here is a portion of her Last Will & Testament: "I leave you love. I leave you hope. I leave you the challenge of developing confidence in one another. I leave you respect for the use of power. I leave you faith, I leave you racial dignity and I leave you the desire to live harmoniously with one another." These simple truths remind us of what truly matters.

Eloquently written, her words inspire us to reflect on the way we live our lives. Many of us measure ourselves against standards of success that have been defined for us in society. I believe our success standards are personal and should include the values we choose as our compass. Our success in life is personal and tied to our purpose and the meaningful ways in which we make our contributions. As author Valorie Burton explains, "Success is a harmony of purpose, resilience, and joy. It is living our life's purpose and embracing (both) resilience and joy as you do."

Our lives are commonly defined by a title. It may be a few short words. It is naturally added after our name when we are introduced. A title is a societal norm and a way in which others measure our success. Our titles may instill a sense of pride, but they may also be an unfair way in which we and others perceive ourselves. This is especially obvious and painful for someone who is newly retired, someone who has lost their job or someone who is juggling both motherhood and a career. A title can impose expectations on us by others, expectations that we often internalize, expectations that define success and happiness by someone else's standards. Author Patti Digh says, "It is ironic that often our definition of success by our own internal measure is the least successful by anyone else's." This can motivate us to spend our time and energy in areas we think others feel are best. She suggests making a list of outcomes and ensuring that each choice we make meets at least three criteria from the following list: having fun, making money, learning, teaching, meeting new people, and extending kindness to others. In other words, if a project, job or opportunity does not meet at least some of these criteria, then save your energy, vision and passion for something else. The next time someone asks you to focus on a project, event or challenge, pull out your list and make sure it meets half your criteria or say "no, thank you." Create your own personal measures of a successful life, not someone else's.

Success is tied to fulfilling a purpose, doing meaningful work and often comes in small but significant experiences and exchanges with others. It is personal. It includes tender moments that give our lives deeper meaning. It is easy to get wrapped up in the spectacular, showy things, but it is the zillion little, personal things just waiting to be cherished that make life special.

Chapter 7

Rejuvenate

Successful people know that to have the freedom and energy to fully enjoy life, good health is necessary. Performing at your very best requires that you take care of your mental, physical and emotional health. Maintaining your health is a baseline for longevity. In fact, it is included in Maslow's hierarchy of basic needs, along with food, shelter, safety and security. Yet prioritizing healthy choices and wellness in our daily lives is a challenge for many of us.

Balance and Prioritize

"The challenge is not to be perfect …
it's to be whole."
Jane Fonda

Staying steadfast and calm in a complicated, fast-paced world is challenging. Stress has become a way of life for many of us, even to the degree that we fail to recognize it. And at times, we present it as a badge of honor. Someone recently remarked to me that they had not had a vacation in nine years. Their wartime medal for all work and no play was worn with pride. Along their journey they must have sensed that people were impressed by their martyrism. Their show of self-sacrifice and willingness to suffer was admired. But the reality is that we need balance between our personal life, our professional life and our family life.

It is important to focus on what we are passionate about, but one aspect of our lives, such as work, should not dominate the others. Different areas of our lives will tip the scales at different times, but maintaining an equilibrium between career, family, volunteer work, civic engagement, wellness activities, hobbies and a social investment in friends is important. Balancing your professional life and your personal life can be a give and take, pushing and pulling you in different directions. That tug of war can be difficult.

My husband and I realized we were saying yes to social events so often that our social time was no longer fun because it was too demanding. We made a new year's resolution pact with each other. We decided we would not schedule ourselves for evening functions two nights in a row. It was a wise decision for us and created a much better balance. Set your own rules and adhere to your own imposed boundaries. And remember, there is no need to apologize.

Although creating a framework for work-life balance requires concentrated effort, it enhances your productivity. This ability to complete tasks and responsibilities efficiently will ultimately provide more time for other commitments.

One way to increase your productivity is to remove digital distractions. The repeated drumbeat encouraging us to unplug is continual for a reason: it is hard to do. Technology is efficient, effective and timesaving. But it can also be pervasive, distracting, addictive and harmful. When we purposely unplug and walk away, we allow ourselves to feel the breeze, soak in the sun, notice the season and focus on the natural beauty around us. Turn off smartphone notifications. "Opting out" of notifications breaks our "always on" mindset. Approach your social media with a "less-is-more" mindset. Consider unfollowing negative or unhealthy posts. Also consider reducing your own number of posts. One of the most common distractions is the obligation we feel to connect with those who have engaged with our content. Minimize other distractions by unsubscribing to any emails that are promotional. Consider a separate email for all purchasing. This will reduce the clutter, junk mail and a crowded inbox that slows you down as you search for important messages. Block off time for email. Read and respond to email when you choose, with appropriate response times, but not necessarily the moment they land in your inbox. Do not feel handcuffed to someone else's schedule. Likewise, do not feel obligated to answer a cell phone call or a text message if you are in the middle of a project or engaged in a conversation with someone. Remember, your undivided attention and your focus on "being in the moment" will result in more satisfying experiences.

Highly positive people lead a well-rounded life. Devote time to all the core areas of your life: career, love, family, friends, self-care, recreation, hobbies and charitable causes. These are all important aspects of your life. Allowing one area of your life to overshadow all the others can leave you feeling unfulfilled.

Find Quiet Time and a Quiet Space

"When I'm tired, I rest. I say,
'I can't be a superwoman today.'"
Jada Pinkett Smith

In today's world, we are rarely given the opportunity to "mull things over" or "think things through." Finding stasis in our busy lives and opportunities to think and reflect can be achieved by balancing the scales with moments of isolation and quiet time. Creating space so that we can reevaluate our perspective while managing our emotional reactivity is not easy but is worth the effort. Calmness can be as contagious as emotionally charged anxiety. We can infect others around us with either.

Investing your efforts in mindfulness as a part of your daily life is well worth your time. Small changes in this area can elevate your positivity. Mindfulness means paying attention in a specific way. It means paying attention purposefully, in the moment and in a nonjudgmental way about ourselves. It is a skill that often requires instruction and certainly requires practice. Systematically building moments of quiet time into our lives, whether meditation or mindfulness, can be centering and provides a place where we gain clarity. It is time devoted to an issue, a problem or a situation where we are isolated from distraction or input by others. It allows us the time and space we need to prepare for our work ahead.

Be still, be quiet. Feel your breath. Relax your body. These set the stage to practice mindfulness and meditation. It is harder to accomplish than it sounds. It requires practice. As author Brené Brown shares, "Stillness is not about focusing on nothingness; it is about creating a clearing. It is opening up an emotionally clutter-free space and allowing ourselves to feel and think and dream and question." This process begins by creating an environment that lends itself to more introspection, more balance and more time to think. Focus on how you spend the first hour of each day. During that golden hour, follow a routine that nurtures you mentally and physically. Enjoy the sunrise, walk your dog or sit quietly and prioritize what you want to accomplish that day. Linger in moments that are beautiful and quiet – a sunrise, a sunset, a pond, a forest, an ocean. These moments will set the tone for the entire day and when repeated in the evening can wrap up the end of your day nicely.

Certain activities create an atmosphere that facilitates our centering and stress relief. For instance, the art of enjoying teatime. The act of brewing, steeping and sipping a hot cup of tea helps us to slow down and take a break. The Eastern world has long known the healing powers of the tea ceremony. Chamomile, mint, lavender and rose teas are particularly known for their relaxing properties. Along with hot tea, add to your regimen bath oils, room sprays, candles and soaps in these same scents. All of these have calming effects and are a great way to introduce a moment of peacefulness into your daily routine.

Quiet isolation can also provide productive opportunities in the workplace. If you work in an office environment, close the door occasionally. Valuable time can easily be wasted with interruptions. Announce to coworkers that the office door will be closed so that you can complete a project. Let them know when the door will reopen. Reopening the door when you commit to doing so will establish a pattern that allows you and your associates to count on your comradery but also gives you the opportunity to complete critical, time-sensitive projects.

Finding quiet time at home in order to read or write can be enhanced by creating a special place, much like a "prayer corner." Create or choose a specific area of your home, a special chair or desk reserved for your seclusion. Writing or journaling can be a constructive way to articulate your thoughts. Having a special place to do this will encourage the process. Taking quiet time to memorialize your thoughts in writing can bring clarity.

"Catching up" with ourselves gives us a sense of being centered, which can motivate us to tackle our next big project or initiative. The premeditated act of sleeping-in on occasion, without setting an alarm, is rejuvenating. Sitting outside on the back porch for your first slow sips of morning coffee is another way. When we have a hectic week or weekend, I reserve the next day as a "Nancy Day." I announce my decree to anyone who may want to infringe on my time. It is my hope that everyone considers me as having flown away to my nest, which I think of as similar to a bird's – a warm, safe, secluded place hidden from all the fuss of the world around me.

There was a time when my entire life seemed to be one big errand. My schedule had a clutter issue. Now I advise, "Replace every possible errand with a delivery." Many of us, years ago, discovered the value of home delivery. It is a way to prevent menial tasks from controlling our daily lives.

Successful people know how to relax and have fun. Joyful people experience the bliss of being engaged – embracing the moment – being "all in." We know it is essential. Taking breaks to recharge your batteries by enjoying all that your life offers right this moment and taking time to think and "catch up" with yourself will give you a sense of fulfillment, which then motivates you to tackle the next big project or initiative.

In Raymond Kethledge and Michael Erwin's book *Lead Yourself First: Inspiring Leadership Through Solitude* they state, "Solitude is a state of mind, a space where you can focus on your own thoughts without distraction, with a power to bring mind and soul together in clear-eyed conviction. Solitude can enhance clarity, spur creativity, sustain emotional balance, and generate the moral courage necessary to overcome adversity and criticism." Have the discipline to unplug. It defies the noise around you. It shows your determination to improve your own clarity by giving yourself the chance to sort through information overload. Decisions often require a process of weighing pros and cons. The decisions we make are based on criteria we must be willing to carefully analyze. This process requires time and structured thinking. In *Lead Yourself First*, retired four-star Marine Corps General James Mattis states, "An effective leader is the person who can maintain their balance and reflect when a lot of people around them are reacting. If I was to sum up the single biggest problem of senior leadership in the information age, it's a lack of reflection."

Solitude also allows us to draw on our intuition. It sets a mood that lets us concentrate on our past and present experiences, removing ourselves from the clamor in our lives. My husband says his best thinking occurs in the shower, where he is protected from interference and disruption. It is warm, refreshing and filled with the water's white noise that allows nothing to distract his thinking. You can find your own place protected from interference, perhaps at a park, on the beach or on the back porch where you hear thoughts whispered only by yourself. It can be any place that does not demand from you your focus. This quiet space gives you the time you need to be creative. It gives you an opportunity to gain perspective and the clarity to see a situation in a larger context. You are better able to craft your responses, identify solutions and clarify action plans. It allows you to be more proactive and less reactive. You can create a positive response of plans, necessary preparation, action and goals. There is the grace that comes with handling a situation rationally. We often fail to give ourselves the space and solitude we need to address a situation appropriately. Create some distance from what is happening around you to ensure you are poised for good decision-making.

Unexpected adversity can create emotional turbulence in our lives. Reflection helps us manage our response so that we are less likely to react emotionally, less likely to have our response deemed a knee-jerk reaction – one without proper thought. The old admonition to "count to ten" still applies, but perhaps we should amend it to "give yourself a quiet space in lieu of counting to one thousand." Step out of the sweeping events of your life to contemplate whatever requires your attention and thought. As my mother used to say, "Let me think on it." Giving yourself quiet time is a strategy to regain emotional balance.

A traditional Navajo teaching says, "When you're out of sorts, sit on the earth. Connect with it." Just sitting still for a while can help us transform negative emotional energy into positive outcomes. Kethledge and Erwin share a story told by Doug Conant, CEO of Campbell Soup Company, who also worries that leaders today do not reflect enough. "Every morning," he says, "for thirty minutes, I sit in the garden or in a comfortable chair with a cup of coffee reflecting. I think about five things: my family, my work, my community, my faith and my personal well-being."

That is a great framework for reflective

thinking. Identify the important aspects of your life that you want to devote time and attention to in the coming months. Reflect on where your focus should be, what needs to change or perhaps to whom you could show more gratitude. This reflective process reminds us what is most important in our lives and allows us to reevaluate our priorities, both professionally and personally. As Brené Brown shares, "Solitude is not the reward for great leadership. It's the path to great leadership."

Combine Physical Activity with an Appreciation for Nature

"Take a breather. Step away from your device.
Get up, get moving, get outside!"
Aliza Sherman

Nature is both soothing and healing. It puts our senses in order. For me, there is nothing more peaceful and more glorious than being outside as the sun sets. As author Barbara Fredrickson shares, "Natural environments may be as important to flourishing as social environments." Her recommendation, "Go outside." Daily physical activity and exercise are essential to reducing stress and maintaining good health. Physical activity, which increases the release of endorphins, combined with mindfulness practices while on a walk in nature is a proven healthy blend. Together they will help you feel happy and more peaceful. "A walk in nature walks the soul back home," says author Mary Davis.

Studies show that people who spend at least twenty minutes outside when the weather is nice have more expansive and open thinking. They demonstrate an increase in positivity. When we immerse ourselves in nature we are drawn to the richness, the diversity and the panorama that nature provides. Nature triggers our fascination. The uniqueness of nature has mystique that arouses our curiosity. Nature is healing and restorative.

Creating an exercise routine surrounded by nature as part of your daily or weekly regimen is challenging. I prefer to think of it as movement – it sounds so much more enjoyable and allows you to start slowly. Begin by walking. Not briskly, not far. Choose scenery you enjoy; perhaps a park, a lake or the ocean. Focus on the colors you see, the sounds of nearby birds or the smell of wet grass after a rainfall. Once you realize that this is *your* time, raise the bar and challenge yourself to increase the length, the pace or the incline. Then balance this with moments of outdoor meditation. But do not be hard on yourself when you fall back to a slower pace for a day or skip a day to complete a project. Stay positive, let go of the minor setbacks and stay focused on the bigger picture: your overall good health and wellness. Physical exercise helps you release nervous energy, which helps you restore yourself emotionally. Exercising in natural surroundings outside can help you gain perspective and find inspiration.

Organize and Declutter to Reduce Stress

"Outer order contributes to inner calm."
Gretchen Rubin

According to Zen organizer Regina Leeds, home and life organization can be broken down into three steps. She calls it her magic formula. Eliminate – Categorize – Organize. Clutter takes up space and closes in on you. Decluttering is a stress reliever. A lack of clutter is Zen. Just like white space in an effective advertisement, lack of clutter allows us to focus on what is important without distractions. Advertisements crammed with text leave us feeling overwhelmed and confused about the message. We tune out. Our home or office can do the same. "Physical clutter is mental clutter. Your space is a tool and you can wield that tool to your advantage," according to author Emily Ley. Simplifying our lives creates space to see what really matters.

To eliminate clutter, start by throwing out stacks of unread magazines, newspapers and other publications. Seeing a stack of unread publications is a source of stress that can translate into negative self-talk. You feel unproductive. The higher the stack, the more overwhelming it is. Discarding the stack feels liberating. Decluttering your space is freeing. Chances are one week later you will not even remember what was in the stack.

To eliminate clutter, throw out everything that's broken, outdated, disliked or useless to you. Your physical space impacts your contentment. It should inspire you, not stress you out or depress you. I have seen offices and homes with stacks of old computer accessories, outdated mobile devices and broken office equipment. Give away all usable items to a charity thrift store. If you are in financial need, take the items that may have value to a consignment store or sell them on eBay if they are worth the effort.

Organize storage areas such as closets, drawers, shelves and cabinets. Closets are the best place to start as they tend to become crammed with clothing. Clean your closet as two seasons approach: In the spring, go through your spring and summer wardrobe. Any item you did not wear the previous spring/summer, give away. Do this in the fall for your fall/winter wardrobe. If you did not wear it last year, you will not wear it this year. Of course, you will rationalize exceptions. "What if I am invited to a luau? Or a '70s party? I will need this shirt or that skirt." Sure, there is a chance you will be invited to a luau or a '70s party. But there is always an opportunity to dress the theme by borrowing from a friend or purchasing from a consignment shop.

My recommendation – let it go.

Once your closet contains only the clothes you wear and enjoy, create a system to be able to find and enjoy your clothes. Place similar items together (pants, blouses, dresses). Then organize them by color, light to dark. Handbags placed on a shelf can also be arranged from light to dark. For an extra level of organization, sort your blouses with short sleeves together and those with long sleeves together. Do this for shoes as well: sandals together, heels together, boots together. If it is affordable, buy felt or plastic hangers all in the same color. Buy extra so that your system can stay intact through the years. It will give your closet an extra boost of Zen.

Sorting and categorizing items as well as labeling storage bins in storage areas allows you to clearly see what you have when it is needed. Think of the stores you shop in; whether it is a grocery store or a clothing store, all the merchandise is offered by category. If you need pickles, you go to that section of an aisle in a grocery store. If you need men's shoes, you go to that section of a department store. Even shopping online is done by category. You enter a retail website and are given a menu of options – categories. They have sorted their inventory for you. You can follow suit in your home by reevaluating each space and storing like items together. In addition, avoid overpacking any closet or cabinet. Picture the cabinets in a vacation rental.

Those rental units do not have kitchen cabinets jam-packed with chipped coffee cups or bathroom closets stuffed with towels. Emulate their closets and cabinets: they have just enough but not too much. They are organized, neat and clean.

Organize your home and workspace around preferences or repeated activity. Dedicate a drawer in the kitchen for frequently used utensils and a cabinet for frequently used pots and pans. Set up office files to easily find the files you need most often. As an example, years ago I realized I was putting monthly bills in files scattered among non-bill files. (I am sure there are millennials reading this thinking, "Who keeps paper files?") I realized if I separated my monthly bill files from all other files and placed them at the front of a file cabinet drawer it would drastically reduce my filing time as I went to those specific files every month. Timesaving organizational practices are worth the effort to employ. As author Regina Leeds says, "I believe that an organized life enables one to have more time, less aggravation, better health, and a chance to accomplish more."

Keep a variety of supplies on hand to improve your organizational uniformity and efficiency. Always keep a stock of items that are necessary at critical times, such as batteries, lightbulbs and cleaning supplies. Keep stamps and return address labels in an easy-to-access box. Keep a box of assorted greeting cards on hand (birthdays, weddings, sympathy, etc.). For traveling, keep necessary toiletries and an extra, stocked makeup bag in your carry-on bag, ready to go. As you prepare for an upcoming trip, create a travel corner at home where you can begin to place the things you would regret leaving behind. These could include electronics, prescriptions and medicines, passports or even an outfit you want to be sure to wear for a special occasion. In addition, as a good organizational practice for travelers, just as I am leaving our home for a trip, I ask myself what would be disastrous or highly disappointing if left behind. That single question has been a lifesaver in the past.

Declutter smartphones by keeping only the apps you consistently use on the main screen. Sort other apps by category and have a screen page for each, such as sports, travel and stores/shopping. Limit online alerts, whether they are on your phone or on your email, and eliminate notifications. Calm yourself with gentle ringtones. Rethink the sounds that you are allowing to fill your space. Sirens, blaring signals and obnoxious noises may not be helping you maintain your equanimity.

Holiday decoration storage may also be overwhelming. If there is one holiday that you go all out on, such as Christmas, create an organizational system that streamlines both the decoration process and returning the decorations to storage. First, purchase all the same style containers to organize your decorations and label them, such as tree lights, table arrangements, tree ornaments, garland, etc. When you begin to decorate, start early and reevaluate each item or container. Is there a Christmas decoration you bemoan each year when you unpack it? Time to give it away. Once the holiday ends, return décor in categories to their respective containers.

One last organization tip is a gift for those you will leave behind one day: Create a binder or a pocket folder that details your final arrangements. My husband and I chose large red binders labeled with our names. Inside are sections with printed tabs: our wills, trusts, durable power of attorney, living wills, funeral arrangements, cemetery mausoleum deeds and critical original documents, such as our birth certificates, our marriage license, car titles and the deed to our home. We hope it provides a roadmap to finalize our personal affairs.

Obligate Your Calendar Carefully

"Never be a slave to an
unrealistically crowded calendar."
Alexandra Stoddard

Take a good look at your calendar. Study each week for the next several months. Divide commitments on the calendar into categories to analyze those you may need to consider canceling. What is

competing for your time and talent – volunteer organizations, social functions, charity events, work,
errands? Ask if each one is necessary and if it brings
joy. Ask if you have committed to it out of obligation. If you do not enjoy it, if it is not crucial to the
goals you want to achieve, if you have agreed to
something only out of obligation, then cross it out.
Remove it from your calendar and notify others involved if necessary.

Circling back and bowing out of obligatory events or meetings gives you the precious gift
of time to focus on projects and people that matter
most to you. In the future, perhaps create a reminder with a sign in your office or a screensaver on your
computer that says, "Obligate Your Calendar Carefully!" Recently I experienced this form of obligation when I was invited to a social event. I realized
I had said yes without thinking. Saying no seemed
to require an appropriate excuse. But an invitation
is just that – an invitation. As Alexandra Stoddard
says, "It is the act of asking for your presence and
participation – a command performance." I have
learned to say, "I will try to be there, but I can't be
certain I can attend." I have even learned to state
matter-of-factly, "I'm sorry but I can't. Lowell and I
have made an important commitment to each other
not to obligate ourselves two nights in a row."

What I have learned is that my time at home
with my husband Lowell and working on projects I

am passionate about is important to me and I need to protect my calendar in order to devote time to these priorities. So often, we say yes to a commitment that interrupts the time we had planned to tackle a project or just simply enjoy peaceful moments at home. Make a choice to spend your precious resource – time – in a way that is fulfilling, in a way that helps you achieve your goals and in a way that brings you contentment. This transformation can create more energy and optimism in your life. It gives you permission to be in greater control of your own time.

In *Psychology Today*, Dr. Shoba Sreenivasan and Dr. Linda Weinberger describe this attitude toward obligations as emotional nourishment: "Another issue for people who always say 'yes' is to consider that saying 'no' to others (e.g., older aged children, work subordinates) can be very healthy for those involved. It may help them develop trial-and-error learning and a sense of responsibility, independence and initiative." Not only is saying no helpful for others, it can also be eye-opening and liberating for you. Growing up, I remember hearing my mother exclaim, "If you want something done right, do it yourself." But trying to do everything yourself or for everyone else obligates you in a way that can be stifling to others. It is the antithesis of learning to delegate. As author Regina Leeds shares, "The word no is now part of my vocabulary. I no longer seek to be loved and accepted by sacrificing myself to others. My physical, mental and emotional needs are important to me."

Eliminate the Hurry in Your Life

"It turns out that, not surprisingly, mastering the art of slowing down doesn't happen quickly. Learning the wisdom of slowing down, of truly living, is itself a journey. But it is also a prescription for better health."
Arianna Huffington

As I was standing in a Starbucks line waiting to order my vanilla latte, a woman turned to me and said, "Chapter 5 is all about you." I had rushed in (long before the days of mobile ordering) and was noticeably in a hurry. "You should read Chapter 5 – An Unhurried Life: The Practice of "Slowing." It's about the benefits of slowing down," she continued. It is a chapter in John Ortberg's book *The Life You've Always Wanted*.

In the book, Ortberg tells this story: "A wise spiritual mentor was asked by a man who wasn't feeling fulfilled, 'What should I be doing differently?' His life seemed empty even though he was so busy. After a long pause, the wise spiritual mentor said, 'Ruthlessly eliminate the hurry in your life.' Seemingly unsatisfied with that, he said, 'okay, what else?' Another long pause. 'There is nothing else.'"

Hurry can keep us from living well. Haste makes waste. We speed, we make mistakes and we do not enjoy the moment. As Carl Jung wrote, "Hurry is not of the devil, hurry is the devil." We believe that if we hurry, we will gain time. That is a myth. Hurry results from trying to multitask. It results from attempting to prepare at the last minute. And worse yet, rushing makes us rude. How can we resolve this situation? Begin by slowing down and performing one task at a time. Engage fully in conversations. Show people they are important to you.

I was once that person who calculated what I could accomplish with the ten minutes I had to spare before arriving at a meeting on time. I could swing through the bank drive-through or stop to pick up the dry-cleaning – even though it made no real difference in my life whether my errands were completed before or after the meeting and most likely whether they were accomplished that day or not. I would enter a meeting feeling harried, self-conscious and disorganized. I was *that* person who unknowingly disguised my lack of preparation with comments about a long traffic light or the unexpected amount of traffic on the road.

The flip side was that when I began arriving early to meetings, I noticed I had a sense of self-confidence I did not have when I tried to make myself invisible while slithering in after a meeting had begun. I noticed the advantage of arriving early. It allowed me to chat with individuals I had a desire to build a relationship with. And I was, in most cases, able to choose my seat. This let me evaluate the best seat – near the front, yet near the coffee – and most importantly, who I could sit near that would be fun, helpful and positive. A vice president of a large national corporation told me once, "I arrive ten minutes early to meetings and learn more about what is really going on in our company than during the entire meeting itself."

Promptness is considerate and thoughtful. It is seen as a positive character trait. It is admired and respected. Arriving early honors the meeting (or any event) and the person hosting the meeting. It communicates that you value the meeting, the chair and the organization. Being late not only devalues and insults the organization and its members, it sends a message to others that you are not in control of your time, your schedule, maybe even your life. It sends a message that other matters are more important.

A former Dean of Students at The Ohio State University facilitated the freshman student orientation during the summer months before the start of the fall semester. I was among fourteen students, out of hundreds who applied, chosen to assist with all aspects of the program. It was a logistical feat to determine who was assigned to each task throughout any given day during the short six weeks as we hosted 8,000 students. Every Sunday we gathered as a group for a staff meeting where our leaders conducted a variety of training classes in subjects such as presentation skills, conflict management and emergency management. They also distributed our assignments, matching us with a variety of programs that would fully initiate freshmen and ensure they felt a sense of belonging. On the rare occasion that someone was late to our team meeting, we were taught an effective lesson by the Dean: "Let's say someone arrives five minutes late. That person didn't waste five minutes of time, they wasted five minutes times the number of people in the meeting. So, if ten people were in attendance for the meeting and you arrive five minutes late, you have wasted fifty minutes. Be dependable – be early."

Take Care of Yourself

"If you think taking care of yourself is
selfish, change your mind.
If you don't, you're simply ducking
your responsibilities."
Ann Richards

We have all heard the announcement: "In the event of a loss in cabin pressure, an oxygen mask will drop from the ceiling compartment above you. Please secure your own mask before assisting others." The same script is repeated on airlines around the world, often ignored by passengers listening to music, reading magazines or using their phones. But the truth is, we have approximately eighteen seconds to perform this task for our bodies to continue to function. So, there is a reason they instruct us to place our own mask on first, before helping our seat companion. In other words, we will be of no use to others if we are not in a healthy state ourselves. I believe this should apply to all aspects of our health. How can we help others to the best of our ability if our own physical, mental or emotional health is neglected?

Happily, we take care of others as a parent, a teacher, a friend, a sibling or a partner, often ignoring our own needs, perhaps due to guilt, martyrism or the fear of being labeled selfish. Author Patti Digh said, "We find diversions from caring for ourselves. If I focus on you, I do not have to focus on myself."

We perform at our very best and can help those around us perform better if we are in top condition. Good health comes from balance and balance comes from moderation. It means eliminating extremes. Julia Childs shared, "Moderation. Small helpings. Sample a little bit of everything. These are the secrets of happiness and good health." There is a famous quote (author unknown) that describes the positive balance in this way: more kindness, less judgment; more jokes, less criticism; more water, less soda; more vegetables, less meat; more outdoors, less monitor time and more love, less anger.

To ward off daily stress, in addition to adding physical activity and bringing nature into your day, start with other simple additions to your life. Anticipate hunger pangs by purchasing healthy snacks as your go-to foods. Drink plenty of water. Develop daily habits that include deep breathing and body stretches before sitting at your computer. In her book *Grace, Not Perfection: Embracing Simplicity, Celebrating Joy*, Emily Ley says it this way: "We can't draw water from an empty well. And when we are empty, we are good for no one. Fill your heart and mind and body with goodness, healthy food, water, rest, and truth. Worry, anxiety, the need for control and the chase of perfection zap the life, energy and health from our bodies."

Get some sleep! Sleep deprivation can increase stress, reduce your focus and make you irritable. Your body is designed to be energetic and active, then it recovers and rejuvenates itself by going to sleep. If you have trouble sleeping soundly, regular body massages can improve sleep quality. They help release tension, reduce stress and lower anxiety levels. A massage increases your body's blood flow, which in turn relaxes you. It also triggers the release of serotonin, a neurotransmitter that can help you feel calm. I call it uninterrupted bliss.

Lighten Up and Laugh

"Dance. Smile. Giggle. Marvel. Trust. Hope.
Love. Wish. Believe. Most of all,
enjoy every moment of the journey, and appreciate
where you are at this moment instead of
always focusing on how far you have to go."
Mandy Hale

"If you could choose one characteristic that would get you through life, choose a sense of humor!" says author Jennifer Jones. When we laugh with others, it is communal, it creates a human connection. It bonds us because it is a shared spontaneous response that is positive and fun. As Brené Brown said, "Laughter, song and dance create emotional and spiritual connections; they remind us of the one thing that truly matters when we are searching for comfort, celebration, inspiration or healing."

Laughter can release the tension we feel from the pressure to be cool and in control. We can be so caught up trying to manage the perceptions of others that we often forget the release that comes with a good laugh. Unleashing our laughing, goofy-dancing selves allows others to do the same. It creates a more honest relationship because it is authentic. It is who we are. Brown shared that the Hopi Indians have a saying: "To watch us dance is to hear our hearts speak."

Years ago, I listened to a cassette tape, "Lighten Up and Laugh." The fact that I heard this message on a cassette tape tells you how long ago I listened to it and how impactful the message was. I would constantly remind myself of the narrator's *Seven Ways to Lighten Up in a Stressed-Out Life*. Her advice changed my life although, sadly, I have no idea who she was. She said, "Lighten Up – Giggle at Yourself; Light the Way – Smile at Yourself and Others; Step Lightly – Skip Around; Discover Your Inner Light – Be Quiet, Meditate; Find the Bless in the Mess; Pleasure Yourself – Enjoy Food, Music and Art; Lighten Your Load – You Don't Have to Do It All; Become a Beam of Light – Spread Joy and Have Fun."

Laughter lets us relax and helps us cope. It is equivalent to aerobic exercise in that it reduces stress hormones and stimulates heart and blood circulation. "A smile starts on the lips, a grin spreads to the eyes, a chuckle comes from the belly; but a good laugh bursts forth from the soul, overflows, and bubbles all around," author Carolyn Birmingham said. Embracing humor sparks energy and enthusiasm in others. It is a positive force in an organization's culture. The atmosphere created in an environment that encourages fun supports successful outcomes. A fun work environment consistently ranks among the top ten reasons why employees enjoy their work.

According to Daniel Goleman, author of *Primal Leadership: Realizing the Power of Emotional Intelligence,* "Humor – workplace jokes and laughter – help to stimulate employee creativity and improve communication and trust." Outstanding leaders tend to be witty. Even in negotiations, friendly banter increases the likelihood that both parties will enjoy consummating the deal. Years ago, my husband purchased two cemeteries from a friend and colleague. They had come to an impasse in their negotiations due to a $17,000 tax bill that would need to be assumed by either the buyer or the seller. Both thought it should be the responsibility of the opposite party. Then Lowell said, "How lucky do you feel?" Our friend responded, "Well, I'm having a pretty good day." Lowell suggested they flip a coin for the tax bill. Both parties' attorneys warned against such behavior. Ultimately, they did flip a coin and Lowell won. Our friends reminisce about those negotiations as often as we do and each time we share a laugh.

Become a Pet Parent

"Having a pet will bless you with many of the happiest days of your life, and one of the worst."
Unknown

Hang out with your hounds. "I think having

an animal in your life makes you a better human," said celebrity cook Rachael Ray. And she is right. Studies show that time spent with our pets is excellent for our physical and mental health. According to Michele Bender, animal advocate and columnist, a University at Buffalo (State University of New York) study asked individuals to complete a difficult task under three scenarios – with their spouse in the room, with their dog in the room and while they were alone. They found that stress levels were the lowest when the pooch was present.

More than 71 million American households (62 percent) have a pet, and most people think of their pets as members of the family. Research studies have found that people who have a pet have healthier hearts. They get more exercise. They stay home from work due to illness less often. They make fewer visits to the doctor. They are less depressed. Pets provide opportunities for social interactions, physical exercise and mental stimulation.

Our pets improve our heart health by reducing our stress, which in turn lowers blood pressure and regulates our heart rate. Studies indicate that having a dog or cat lowers the risk of heart disease as well as lowering stress, which contributes to improved health. Children's exposure to companion animals also eases anxiety. Studies indicate that when a pet dog is present, children have lower blood pressure, lower heart rates and less behavioral distress.

Specific impacts on physical health suggest that the social support a pet provides can make a person feel more relaxed. The social support from friends and family can have similar benefits, but interpersonal relationships often cause stress as well, whereas pets may be less likely to cause stress. They love us unconditionally. No matter the type of day we have had, they are overjoyed to see us, and our interaction with them immediately has a positive impact on our mood.

I realized early in our adoption of Snowball, a maltipoo rescue and a four-legged family member, that my interaction with strangers changed when she and I took walks together. People who have leashed pets have an expressed agenda: they are walking their dogs and giving both themselves and their pets some healthy outdoor exercise. While out walking, the presence of a pet results in more social interactions with others. In other words, a person with a pet is more trusted and more approachable. Pet ownership, especially among elderly people, may be an important source of social support that enhances overall wellness. The simple gesture of a nod, a smile or a casual greeting reduces feelings of isolation or loneliness and sends a message of acceptance and likeability. Studies indicate that elderly individuals who have a dog or cat are better able to perform certain physical activities deemed "activities for daily living" such as the ability to climb stairs, bend, kneel or stoop. They are more likely to take medication, prepare meals, bathe and dress themselves. Research also suggests that taking care of a pet may give older individuals a sense of responsibility and purpose that contributes to their overall well-being.

"One thing is for sure, dogs are not our whole life, but they make our lives whole," said Roger Caras, wildlife photographer, preservationist and author.

Chapter 8

Love Well

*"Love must be learned and learned
again and again; there is no end to it.
Hate needs no instruction but
waits only to be provoked."*
Katherine Anne Porter

Choose Your Spouse Wisely

*"The single most important career
decision that a woman makes
is whether she will have a life partner
and who that partner is."*
Sheryl Sandberg

I learned a very important philosophy of life from my husband Lowell: "The two most important things in life are the person we choose to spend the rest of our lives with and the career that we love and are passionate about that allows us the opportunity to do whatever we want together. And whatever is third is so far behind the first two, it doesn't matter." So much of our future rests in these two single decisions, particularly the former.

Before meeting Lowell, I remember sensing that my drive and ambition were threatening to other men I had dated. Sheryl Sandberg wrote, "I don't know of one woman in a leadership position whose life partner is not fully – and I mean fully – supportive of her career. No exceptions." My husband believes all women should be strong, decisive and ambitious. He has been my cheerleader. There are enough barriers in our lives. An unsupportive partner or someone who seems threatened by our ambition and success does not need to be one of them.

In healthy relationships, spouses complement one another. Spouses are neither completely alike nor are they opposites. They are each capable human beings, but their strengths lie in different areas. They complement each other, they do not compete. Equally important in healthy relationships is the mindset of both individuals toward being a couple with a commitment to being a good spouse. While I was driving down the freeway in Atlanta as a marketing representative for Eastman Kodak Company, I happened to hear on the car radio Dr. James Dobson with *Focus on the Family*. He said, "Couples first fall in love, then they decide to love." I believe Lowell and I both shared that unspoken knowledge that we not only fell in love but decided to love. Research psychologist and couples counselor John Gottman explains in his book *What Makes Love Last: How to Build Trust and Avoid Betrayal* that forty years of research determined trust and commitment are crucial to holding relationships together: "When both partners have a strong commitment to a relationship, this leads to a strong sense of trust, which makes love last."

Be the Best Companion You Can Be

"The best thing to hold onto in life is each other."
Audrey Hepburn

I believe there are three keys to a successful marriage or relationship. The first is to appreciate the other person. The best relationships outwardly express a high degree of appreciation. Appreciation is demonstrated each time you keenly notice and express to your partner a sense of gratitude for something they have done for you. Those who appreciate their partner are likely to feel more appreciated by their partner in return. If you focus on being the best companion you can be, it starts with yourself. You cannot love someone else if you do not love yourself. As author Emily Ley said, "You can't embrace someone else's imperfections until you have embraced your own."

Second, give compliments to each other both directly and to others while your partner is present.

Be each other's cheerleaders. Encourage each other. Be happy and excited for each other's successes. In the best relationships, partners express their fondness and admiration for each other.

Affection is the third key. Demonstrate deep care for each other. Spend as much time together as possible. Plan regular time together and create traditions such as date nights or candlelight dinners. Although having your separate hobbies and passions is healthy, be inquisitive about each other's activities. Demonstrating genuine interest, empathy and concern will support and help facilitate harmony in your relationship.

To be your happiest, be certain your mindset is positive about your relationship and the role you play in it. Ensuring you convey positivity will result in experiencing the positive. Brené Brown, professor and author, explains, "We know what matters, but who we are matters more. Those who feel lovable, who love and who experience belonging simply believe they are worthy of love and belonging." This positivity translates into shared moments of joy and laughter that deepen a relationship. In sharing your positivity with your spouse or partner, through humor, fun-loving moments and approving smiles, you convey that you are moving forward together. You are building and strengthening your connection.

If you do not give 100 percent in your relationship, you will always assume your partner is not giving 100 percent either. If you want the relationship to be built on trust, you must be a trustworthy partner. Being honest in the relationship holds your partner accountable to do the same. It allows both of you to continually think about your choices and how they can help (or hurt) your partner and your relationship.

Keys to Happiness

*"If your home environment is good
and peaceful and easy, your life
is better and easier."*
Lori Greiner

I believe the key to happiness is to focus on being an inspiration to others, focus on sharing joy and laughter with those you love and focus on something you look forward to with anticipation and excitement. If you were asked, "Are you living well?" your answer would depend on several factors: health, financial situation, career status, work life, professional relationships, personal relationships and your love life. The litmus test is, "Are you feeling good emotionally?"

When we feel good emotionally, when we experience long-term happiness, we experience many related benefits such as increased productivity and increased self-confidence. But our happiness benefits others, too. A happy person is positive, and that positivity affects others. When someone is referred to as "a ray of sunshine," that person's happiness and positivity is affecting others. As Mother Teresa said, "Spread love everywhere you go. Let no one ever come to you without leaving happier."

A positive attitude coupled with enthusiasm will spread to others and can make an amazing difference in your personal and professional life. People gravitate to positive people rather than avoiding them. Interpersonal relationships flourish because people value the company of positive people. Companies search for leaders who understand that the biggest reason associates like their jobs is the positive attitude and enthusiastic behavior of their immediate supervisor. Motivating others hinges on positivity. Problem-solving hinges on a positive attitude. Positive leaders visualize problems as a challenge that can be overcome. By living well we help others to live well. We can positively influence the atmosphere of a room and we can positively influence another person's life.

The following is the philosophy often attributed to Charles Schulz, the creator of the *Peanuts* comic strip, but has thought to be traced to Dennis Fakes in his book *G.R.A.C.E.: The Essence of Spirituality*. He first asked his audience to answer these questions: Name the five wealthiest people in the world. Name the last five Heisman Trophy winners.

Name the last five winners of the Miss America pageant.

Name ten people who have won the Nobel or Pulitzer Prize.

Name the last half-dozen Academy Award winners for best actor and actress.

Name the last decade's worth of World Series winners.

"It is difficult, yes?" he said. "The point is none of us remember the headliners of yesterday. These are no second-rate achievers. They are the best in their fields. But the applause dies. Awards tarnish. Achievements are forgotten. Accolades and certificates are buried with their owners."

Then he asked his audience to answer these questions:

Name a few teachers who aided your journey through school.

Name three friends who have helped you through a difficult time.

Name five people who have taught you something worthwhile.

Name a few people who have made you feel appreciated and special.

Name five people you enjoy spending time with.

"Easier?" he asked. "The lesson is this: The people who make a difference in your life are not the ones with the most credentials, the most money, or the most awards. They are the ones that care."

Blossom

"Life is a magical journey – live it accordingly."
Unknown

Connect. Engage. Inspire. Lead. Life is about appreciating the significance of the people in our lives. It is about channeling our energy and our passion to create positive contributions. Life is not just about enjoying the journey. Life is about who we share our journey with, how we contribute to the world around us and the ways in which we make a meaningful difference in the lives of others.

In honor of Dr. Mary McLeod Bethune, I would humbly like to leave you with these final thoughts in the way she left us her Last Will & Testament:

I leave you aspiration to continue to learn.

I leave you eagerness to invest lovingly in relationships.

I leave you openness to try new things, meet new people and visit new places.

I leave you encouraged to focus on positivity.

I leave you inspired to make purposeful and meaningful contributions.

I leave you the commitment to share gratitude and appreciation.

I leave you optimism for your future.

As author Louise Hay advises: "I choose to make the rest of my life the best of my life."

References

American Psychological Association quoted in Jim Taylor, "Technology: Myth of Multitasking." *The Power of Prime* (blog), *Psychology Today*, March 30, 2011.

Baker, Lois. 1999. "Pet Dog or Cat Controls Blood Pressure Better Than ACE Inhibitor, UB Study of Stockbrokers Finds." University at Buffalo (State University of New York), November 7, 1999.

Bethune, Mary McLeod. Mary McLeod Bethune Council House National Historic Site, National Park Service, U.S. Department of the Interior.

Blanchard, Ken, and Claire Diaz-Ortiz. Copyright, Blanchard Family Partnership and Claire Diaz-Ortiz. 2017. *One Minute Mentoring: How to Find and Work with a Mentor and Why You'll Benefit from Being One.* New York: HarperCollins Publishers.

Burns, James MacGregor. 1985. *Leadership.* New York: Harper & Row.

Burns, James MacGregor. 2003. *Transforming Leadership: The New Pursuit of Happiness.* New York: Grove.

Burton, Valorie. 2012. *Successful Women Think Differently: 9 Habits to Make You Happier, Healthier, and More Resilient.* Eugene, OR: Harvest House.

Cain, Susan. 2012. *Quiet: The Power of Introverts in a World That Can't Stop Talking.* New York: Crown.

Cheung, Lilian. 2003. "10 Mindful Ways to Enjoy the Holiday Season." Huffington Post.

Chua, Celestine. 2013. 7 Habits of Highly Positive People: The Secret to Constant Happiness. The Positivity Blog, Henrick Edberg.

Conrad, Charles, and Marshall Scott Poole. 2005. *Strategic Organizational Communication: In a Global Economy.* Belmont, CA: Thomson Wadsworth.

Covey, Stephen R. 2013. *The 7 Habits of Highly Effective People: Powerful Lessons in Personal Change.* New York: Simon & Schuster.

Davis, Mary. 2017. *Every Day Spirit: A Daybook of Wisdom, Joy, and Peace.* Rich River Publishing Company.

Digh, Patti. 2008. *Life is a Verb: 37 Days to Wake Up, Be Mindful, and Live Intentionally.* Guildford, CT: Globe Pequot.

Duckworth, Angela. 2016. *Grit: The Power of Passion and Perseverance.* New York: Scribner.

Dungy, Tony. 2010. *The Mentor Leader: Secrets to Building People and Teams that Win Consistently.* Carol Stream, IL: Tyndale House.

Emmons, Robert A. 2013. *Gratitude Works!: A 21-Day Program for Creating Emotional Prosperity.* Jossey-Bass.

Emmons, Robert A. 2007. *Thanks!: How the New Science of Gratitude Can Make You Happier.* Boston: Houghton Mifflin Harcourt.

Fakes, Dennis. 2001. *G.R.A.C.E.: The Essence of Spirituality.* San Jose: Writer's Showcase Press.

Fenet, Lydia. 2019. *The Most Powerful Woman in the Room is You: Command an Audience and Sell Your Way to Success.* New York: Galley Books, an Imprint of Simon & Schuster, Inc.

Fernandez, Rich. 2016. "5 Ways to Boost Your Resilience at Work." *Harvard Business Review*, June 27, 2016.

Finerman, Karen quoted in Jean Chatzky, "3 Reasons Multitasking is a Huge Waste of Time (and

How to Stop Doing It)." *Forbes*, May 6, 2016.

Fredrickson, Barbara L. 2009. *Positivity: Ground-breaking Research Reveals How to Embrace the Hidden Strength of Positive Emotions, Overcome Negativity, and Thrive.* New York: Crown.

Frei, David. 2011. *Angel on a Leash: Therapy Dogs and Lives They Touch.* Irvine, CA: Bow Tie Press.

Goleman, Daniel, Richard Boyatzis, and Annie McKee. 2002. *Primal Leadership: Realizing the Power of Emotional Intelligence.* Boston: Harvard Business Press.

Gottman, John. 2017. *What Makes Love Last: How to Build Trust and Avoid Betrayal,* New York: Simon & Schuster, quoted in Rachel Gillett, "Power Couples Who Stay Together Have 9 Things in Common." *Independent* (UK), October 23, 2017.

Hawkins, John. 2001. *Leadership as a Lifestyle: The Path to Personal Integrity and Positive Influence.* United States: Executive Excellence Publishing.

Hubbard, Elbert. 2012. "Simplify Your Life, Get Organized, Achieve Your Goals." http://blog.organizetosimplify.com/tag/elbert-hubbard/.

Keller, Gary, and Jay Papasan. 2012. *The One Thing: The Surprisingly Simple Truth Behind Extraordinary Results.* Austin, TX: Bard.

Kethledge, Raymond M., and Michael S. Erwin. 2017. *Lead Yourself First: Inspiring Leadership Through Solitude.* New York: Bloomsbury USA.

Kiyosaki, Robert T. 2017. *Rich Dad Poor Dad: With Updates for Today's World – And 9 New Study Session Sections.* Plata Publishing, LLC.

Kohn, Stephen E., and Vincent D. O'Connell. 2015. *9 Powerful Practices of Really Great Mentors: How to Inspire and Motivate Anyone.* Pompton Plains, NJ: Career.

Leeds, Regina. 2008. *One Year to an Organized Life: From Your Closets to Your Finances, the Week-by-Week Guide to Getting Completely Organized for Good.* New York: MJF Books.

Ley, Emily. 2016. *Grace, Not Perfection: Embracing Simplicity, Celebrating Joy.* Nashville, TN: Thomas Nelson.

Lotich, Patricia. 2019. "How to Be a Good Boss – 10 Qualities of a Good Boss." Thriving Small Business, January 9, 2019.

Lustig, Robert H. 2019. "Don't Be a Pleasure Junkie: Find the Secret to True Happiness." As seen in Bottom Line Personal app for iPad, June 2019.

Maitland, Alison. 2016. "Taking the Helm on the High Seas." *Financial Times*.

Manning, Doug. 2001. *The Funeral*. 2nd ed. Oklahoma City: InSight Books.

Maxwell, John C. 1993. *Developing the Leader within You*. Nashville, TN: Thomas Nelson.

Maxwell, John C. 2008. *Mentoring 101: What Every Leader Needs to Know*. HarperCollins Leadership.

Meyer, Urban. 2015. *Above the Line: Lessons in Leadership and Life from a Championship Season*. New York: Penguin.

Michelli, Joseph A. 2018. *The New Gold Standard: 5 Leadership Principles for Creating a Legendary Customer Experience Courtesy of the Ritz-Carlton Hotel Company*. McGraw-Hill.

Morgan, Nick. 2009. *Trust Me: Four Steps to Authenticity and Charisma*. San Francisco: Jossey-Bass.

Rath, Tom. 2007. *StrengthsFinder 2.0*. Gallup Press.

Rovner, Julie. 2012. "Pet Therapy: How Animals and Humans Heal Each Other." NPR, March 5, 2012.

Sandberg, Sheryl. 2013. *Lean In: Women, Work, and the Will to Lead*. New York: Alfred A. Knopf.

Schieffer, Bob. 2003. *This Just In: What I Couldn't Tell You on TV*. New York: G.P. Putnam's Sons.

Steves, Rick. 2012. "Teaching & History." Lecture, Part I, Gonzaga University, 2011. Posted on YouTube, May 24, 2012.

St. George, Andrew. 2013. "Leadership Lessons from the Royal Navy." McKinsey & Company, January 1, 2013.

Stoddard, Alexandra. 2004. *Things I Want My Daughters to Know: A Small Book About the Big Issues in Life*. New York: HarperCollins.

Thaler, Linda Kaplan, and Robin Koval. 2006. *The Power of Nice: How to Conquer the Business World with Kindness*. New York: Doubleday.

Veenhoven, Ruut. 2016. *Happiness in Nations: Subjective Appreciation of Life in 56 Nations, 1946-1992*.

Walters, Barbara. comfortingquotes.com.

Weems, Mason Locke. 1809. *The Life of Washington.* Philadelphia: Mathew Carey.

Welch, Jack. 2013. "The Six Deadly Sins of Leadership." LinkedIn, March 27, 2013.

Wilks, E.L. 2004. *Chief Servant: The Life and Leadership of Dr. Oswald P. Bronson, Sr., President of Bethune-Cookman College.* St. Augustine, FL: Legacies & Memories.

Wilks, E.L. 2017. *The Lohman Way: Entrepreneur Lowell Lohman's Story and Strategies for Building Multimillion-Dollar Family Businesses.* St. Augustine, FL: Legacies & Memories.

Wolfelt, Alan, 2011. *Creating Meaningful Funeral Experiences, A Guide for Caregivers.* Fort Collins, CO: Companion Press.

Zentis, Nancy. 2008. "Keys to Successful Mentoring Programs." LinkedIn, October 29, 2008.

Appendices

Dr. Mary McLeod Bethune's Last Will and Testament

Sometimes as I sit communing in my study I feel that death is not far off. I am aware that it will overtake me before the greatest of my dreams – full equality for the Negro in our time – is realized. Yet, I face that reality without fear or regrets. I am resigned to death as all humans must be at the proper time. Death neither alarms nor frightens one who has had a long career of fruitful toil. The knowledge that my work has been helpful to many fills me with joy and great satisfaction.

Since my retirement from an active role in educational work and from the affairs of the National Council of Negro Women, I have been living quietly and working at my desk at my home here in Florida. The years have directed a change of pace for me. I am now 78 years old and my activities are no longer so strenuous as they once were. I feel that I must conserve my strength to finish the work at hand.

Already I have begun working on my autobiography which will record my life-journey in detail, together with the innumerable side trips which have carried me abroad, into every corner of our country, into homes both lowly and luxurious, and even into the White House to confer with Presidents. I have also deeded my home and its contents to the Mary McLeod Bethune Foundation, organized in March, 1953, for research, interracial activity and the sponsorship of wider educational opportunities.

Sometimes I ask myself if I have any other legacy to leave. Truly, my worldly possessions are few. Yet, my experiences have been rich. From them, I have distilled principles and policies in which I believe firmly, for they represent the meaning of my life's work. They are the products of much sweat and sorrow.

Perhaps in them there is something of value. So, as my life draws to a close, I will pass them on to Negroes everywhere in the hope that an old woman's philosophy may give them inspiration. Here, then is my legacy.

I LEAVE YOU LOVE. Love builds. It is positive and helpful. It is more beneficial than hate. Injuries quickly forgotten quickly pass away. Personally and racially, our enemies must be forgiven. Our aim must be to create a world of fellowship and justice where no man's skin, color or religion, is held against him. "Love thy neighbor" is a precept which could transform the world if it were universally practiced. It connotes brotherhood and, to me, brotherhood of man is the noblest concept in all human relations. Loving your neighbor means being interracial, interreligious and international.

I LEAVE YOU HOPE. The Negro's growth will be great in the years to come. Yesterday, our ancestors endured the degradation of slavery, yet they retained their dignity. Today, we direct our economic and political strength toward winning a more abundant and secure life. Tomorrow, a new Negro, unhindered by race taboos and shackles, will benefit from more than 330 years of ceaseless striving and struggle. Theirs will be a better world. This I believe with all my heart.

I LEAVE YOU THE CHALLENGE OF DE-VELOPING CONFIDENCE IN ONE ANOTHER. As long as Negroes are hemmed into racial blocks by prejudice and pressure, it will be necessary for them to band together for economic betterment. Negro banks, insurance companies and other business-es are examples of successful, racial economic enterprises. These institutions were made possible by vision and mutual aid. Confidence was vital in getting them started and keeping them going. Negroes have got to demonstrate still more confidence in each other in business. This kind of confidence will aid the economic rise of the race by bringing togeth-er the pennies and dollars of our people and plough-ing them into useful channels. Economic separatism cannot be tolerated in this enlightened age, and it is not practicable. We must spread out as far and as fast as we can, but we must also help each other as we go.

I LEAVE YOU A THIRST FOR EDUCATION. Knowledge is the prime need of the hour. More and more, Negroes are taking full advantage of hard-won opportunities for learning, and the educational level of the Negro population is at its highest point in history. We are making greater use of the privileges inherent in living in a democracy. If we continue in this trend, we will be able to rear increasing numbers of strong, purposeful men and women, equipped with vision, mental clarity, health and education.

I LEAVE YOU RESPECT FOR THE USES OF POWER. We live in a world which respects power above all things. Power, intelligently directed, can lead to more freedom. Unwisely directed, it can be a dreadful, destructive force. During my lifetime I have seen the power of the Negro grow enormously. It has always been my first concern that this power should be placed on the side of human justice.

Now that the barriers are crumbling everywhere, the Negro in America must be ever vigilant lest his forces be marshalled behind wrong causes and undemocratic movements. He must not lend his support to any group that seeks to subvert democracy. That is why we must select leaders who are wise, courageous, and of great moral stature and ability. We have great leaders among us today: Ralph Bunche, Channing Tobias, Mordecai Johnson, Walter White, and Mary Church Terrell. [The latter now deceased]. We have had other great men and women in the past: Frederick Douglass, Booker T. Washington, Harriet Tubman, and Sojourner Truth. We must produce more qualified people like them, who will work not for themselves, but for others.

I LEAVE YOU FAITH. Faith is the first factor in a life devoted to service. Without faith, nothing is possible. With it, nothing is impossible. Faith in God is the greatest power, but great, too, is faith in oneself. In 50 years the faith of the American Negro in himself has grown immensely and is still increasing. The measure of our progress as a race is in precise relation to the depth of the faith in our people held by our leaders. Frederick Douglass, genius though he was, was spurred by a deep conviction that his people would heed his counsel and follow him to freedom. Our greatest Negro figures have been imbued with faith. Our forefathers struggled for liberty in conditions far more onerous than those we now face, but they never lost the faith. Their perseverance paid rich dividends. We must never forget their sufferings and their sacrifices, for they were the foundations of the progress of our people.

I LEAVE YOU RACIAL DIGNITY. I want Negroes to maintain their human dignity at all costs. We, as Negroes, must recognize that we are the custodians as well as the heirs of a great civilization. We have given something to the world as a race and for this we are proud and fully conscious of our place in the total picture of mankind's development. We must learn also to share and mix with all men. We must make and effort to be less race conscious and more conscious of individual and human values. I have never been sensitive about my complexion. My color has never destroyed my self-respect nor has it ever caused me to conduct myself in such a manner as to merit the disrespect of any person. I have not let my color handicap me. Despite many crushing burdens and handicaps, I have risen from the cotton fields of South Carolina to found a college, administer it during its years of growth, become a public servant in the government of our country and a leader of women. I would not exchange my color for all the wealth in the world, for had I been born white I might not have been able to do all that I have done or yet hope to do.

I LEAVE YOU A DESIRE TO LIVE HARMONIOUSLY WITH YOUR FELLOW MEN. The problem of color is worldwide. It is found in Africa and Asia, Europe and South America. I appeal to American Negroes -- North, South, East and West -- to recognize their common problems and unite to solve them.

I pray that we will learn to live harmoniously with the white race. So often, our difficulties have made us hypersensitive and truculent. I want to see my people conduct themselves naturally in all relationships -- fully conscious of their manly responsibilities and deeply aware of their heritage. I want them to learn to understand whites and influence them for good, for it is advisable and sensible for us to do so. We are a minority of 15 million living side by side with a white majority. We must learn to deal with these people positively and on an individual basis.

I LEAVE YOU FINALLY A RESPONSIBILITY TO OUR YOUNG PEOPLE. The world around us really belongs to youth for youth will take over its future management. Our children must never lose their zeal for building a better world. They must not be discouraged from aspiring toward greatness, for they are to be the leaders of tomorrow. Nor must they forget that the masses of our people are still underprivileged, ill-housed, impoverished and victimized by discrimination. We have a powerful potential in our youth, and we must have the courage to change old ideas and practices so that we may direct their power toward good ends.

Faith, courage, brotherhood, dignity, ambition, responsibility -- these are needed today as never before. We must cultivate them and use them as tools for our task of completing the establishment of equality for the Negro. We must sharpen these tools in the struggle that faces us and find new ways of using them. The Freedom Gates are half-ajar. We must pry them fully open.

If I have a legacy to leave my people, it is my philosophy of living and serving. As I face tomorrow, I am content, for I think I have spent my life well. I pray now that my philosophy may be helpful to those who share my vision of a world of Peace, Progress, Brotherhood, and Love.

Used with permission of Bethune-Cookman University.

Acknowledgments

The abundance in my life can be summed up in two words: family and friends. This book was possible because of the love and support I have received from those with whom I share a mutual and unconditional bond.

I begin my acknowledgments with my mother. She returned to school to finish her undergraduate degree at The Ohio State University when I was a teenager. She subsequently earned her master's degree and taught second-grade elementary for twenty-plus years. At sixteen, her first job was as a tour guide and switchboard operator at JM Smucker Company headquartered in Orrville, Ohio, near her hometown. She was a proud Buckeye, she made amazing homemade pies and she was well-read on a variety of subjects. Thank you, mom, for the love that you gave me, for the values you instilled in me and for all you taught me. From you, I have learned more than I can list, and I have tried my best to put these into practice:

I have learned the importance of an education and that lifetime learning is equally valuable.

I have learned not to be afraid to ask questions.

I have learned the love of reading.

I have learned the satisfaction of hard work.

I have learned the importance of good manners.

I have learned to be appreciative and grateful.

I have learned the grace that kindness brings and the healing effects of humor.

I have learned the value of embracing diversity and learning from the world around us.

My drive and ambition have been consistently encouraged by my husband Lowell. He has had the greatest impact on my success. Together with our family, we pursued business ventures that ultimately allowed us to donate our time and treasure to causes we believe in. The journey has been exciting. In our family businesses Lowell soared high above the daily operational details but swooped down like an eagle when we needed his wisdom. His ability to focus on what was most important and let go of details and minutia was an invaluable lesson to me and enabled me to have the opportunity to achieve more. He unselfishly allowed me the time needed to write this book. Lowell spent countless hours downstairs, while I have tucked myself away in "Nancy's Nest." My goal has never wavered, I continue to want to be the best wife and partner I can possibly be.

Thank you, Lowell, for making me your Cinderella and giving me this life which I never would have thought possible. To be living this life and sharing it with someone as loving as you is a dream come true. Thank you for loving me so much. I love you with all my heart.

Ed Wilks – thank you for writing the book *The Lohman Way*. It was beautifully written and provided a platform for us – a springboard for opportunities. We will be forever grateful to you for writing the perfect book for us. During the interviews that helped you gather the information and stories you needed for *The Lohman Way* our relationship grew and led us to conversations about this book. More importantly, they led to your encouragement of this book. You have been an excellent editor. I am grateful for your writing skills, your candor and your patience.

This book would not have been possible without the generous gift of time and talent from my sister Ann. She has provided me with her guidance and wisdom all my life. When I was in fifth grade, I was required to enter the Knights of Columbus essay contest. The essay prompt was "my family is like a little church." When I shared this news with my sister, she immediately gave me an excellent theme for my essay and helped me bring the idea to fruition. I won first place. Fifty-two years later, she continues to share her reflections, philosophies and editing skills with me. She spent hours assisting me with my graduate thesis and has now spent hours helping me create the best results possible for this book.

To both my sisters, Ann and Carolyn – I am the luckiest sister in the world to have you as my sisters. Thank you for loving me as only sisters can. You are witty, smart, genuine and you take acceptance and understanding to a higher level than most. I am so proud of who you are. We lived through our share of childhood dysfunction together and yet we all have an abundance of strong, healthy relationships including supportive, loving husbands. I hope you know I am always right there for you just as you have been for me.

To my family, particularly my bonus sons Ty and Brian who allowed me to be a mother to them; my daughters-in-law Jennifer and Tovah; my brothers-in-law and sisters-in-law Darrin, Rob, Victor, Mary, Daryl, Christine and Linda; my nieces Leanne, Ashley, "HallieB," Méabh, Bébhinn and Lauren; my nephews Andrew, Caolán, Chris and Michael; my grandchildren Taylor, Jordan and Tristen; my great-nieces and great-nephews Chase, Brooklyn, Elise, Eleanor (Ella), Jacob, Caleb, Ella, Raegan and Riley; and those that are extended family of all of you, thank you for the joy that you have brought to our lives. You are all talented in your own ways and it has been amazing to watch you excel in your careers, in sports and through your passions. I am grateful that the youngest in our families are growing up to be educated, independent, interesting, polite and loving. Thank you for allowing me to be your "Mom," your "Aunt Nancy" and your "Grandma Nancy." I treasure our family memories and I know that holidays are more special when we are together.

To my brother Richard, thank you for being who you are. I am not sure I can describe the emotional wholeness I felt when we found each other. I never felt like my life puzzle was complete until now. To meet you and instantly feel your unconditional brotherly love reinforced the notion that a life well lived will be rewarded. It is the ultimate "good karma." I love that you are in our lives. I have learned so much from you, but especially how unconditional love really feels because it was so instantaneous with us. (I learned in my mid-teens from my dad, a few years before he died, that we had a brother in England. We did not know his name or even whether it was true or not, but for forty-three years I had been wondering.)

I am also eternally grateful for a group of close friends I call the "Effervescent Eight." I will focus with pleasure on showing all of you my deep appreciation for our friendship and bond in as many ways as possible. Know that I respect you all tremendously. I am proud to know you and feel privileged to call each of you my friend. I will try to be the greatest friend I can be as we share this journey of life together.

Mary M. – You are my "sista from a different mista." You have been my confidante and my collaborator during family vacations and holiday events. Thank you for your hilarious sense of humor, your dry wit and your allegiance. You can be the life of the party and every family gathering is more fun when you are with us. I treasure our sisterhood.

Susan P. – I admire and respect you tremendously. You are driven, ambitious and resilient. We share the same core values and ideologies, which is remarkably reassuring to me. I am truly thankful for the security in knowing you never waver in your convictions. I marvel at your indomitable spirit, everything that you have accomplished and the amazing woman and leader you have become. Thank you for being a loving and loyal best friend.

Bridget B. – Your positive influence is a weekly and at times daily inspiration to me. You are accepting and compassionate. You are one in a million because you see the positive in everyone. You motivate me to be a better person because of your steadfast outreach to others and your encouragement to focus on health, nutrition and wellness.

Sherry G. – You are creative, artistic and a free spirit – all of which I admire. You are also affectionate and supportive. Above all, you have been a loyal partner with me and have marched side by side with me for many causes, particularly capital campaign fundraising. Your willingness to stand together with me to achieve significant goals has been unfaltering and I will be eternally grateful.

Jill S. – Your enthusiasm is contagious. Every event is more fun when you are there. You are eternally positive. You have reinforced the joy of giving meaningful gifts to others. The gifts you have showered me with over the years bring me daily joy. I am also grateful for your love of photos. It is an extra bonus for me to have a shutterbug buddy who takes and shares as many pictures as I do and deeply loves the Shutterfly books we create.

Kathy C. – Thank you for being fun, loving and such a smart, rational sounding board. You have been a personal safeguard for me with your wise counsel and your thoughtfulness. You are a fine Irish lass. Your communication skills are a lesson in diplomacy each time I am with you and a reminder of how important it is to communicate with kindness.

Joni H. – Thank you for being thoughtful, accepting and supportive. I have learned so much from you in the small window of time we have spent together, and I look forward with a large grin on my face to more shared experiences. You are another friend with the gift of diplomacy and a beautiful influence on the world around you.

Michelle C. – Thank you for reminding through your life's work that if a situation needs to be improved then jump in and do something to make it better. You walk the talk of Mary McLeod Bethune, "If I have a legacy to leave my people, it is my philosophy of living and serving." Thank you for allowing us to talk openly and candidly about social justice. Thank you for helping me be more sensitive and empathetic about what it is like to be black in America. You have taught me so much and you are a wonderful, loving friend.

To the husbands of these wonderful women, Bill S., Bryan B., Carl P., Larry B., Pat R. and Roy G. I love you too and am thankful for you. I am grateful that we all know one another and have the opportunity to share great moments together. I am continually awed and inspired by your professional accomplishments and the community enthusiasts you are. You are strong individuals, and I am grateful that you proudly acknowledge and support the strong women you have married.

Philomene and Erich – Little did we know when we sailed around the world on the Queen Mary 2 maiden voyage that having you as our neighbors in suite 9007 would change our lives forever. It was a trip of a lifetime. Our cruise ship sailed around the globe for eighty days and during that time we grew to love the two of you more and more. You are the most loving people on this earth and have made a tremendous difference in our lives. Thank goodness we sailed over St. Patrick's Day. Our dear mutual friends Mary and Bernard from Cork taught us how to celebrate St. Patrick's Day authentically and that created an unbreakable bond between us that has lasted all this time.

The friends who have touched my life in special ways and taught me valuable life lessons throughout my life deserve a mountain of thanks. Many of you have taught me life's best practices on how to live fully and authentically. Your friendship, our shared experiences and your thoughtful outreach through phone calls and notes, many of which sit inside my gratitude box, mean so much to me. Friendships are made throughout life, but I would like to share a special thank you to Polly Dale, my oldest friend since seventh grade. I have been so lucky to grow up with your kind spirit and loving influence. You are always "right there" in my life like a guardian angel. To Arlene W., Carrie S., Christine D-B., Edgar S., Gale L., Hezi C., Jill S., John and Shelia H., Karole Sue R. (dec'd), Kathi T., Kelly R., Lorry L., Lynne C., Mary C., Renee G., Shawn A., Stephanie M., Sheriff G., Sheryl C., Tina C., Deb S., Valerie H. and to the Ho Ho Ho Girls over the years – Aud O. (dec'd), Denise B., Desi P., Judy C. (dec'd), Judy K., Linda S., Mary B., Mary M., Melinda D., and Rachel M. – I have been profoundly grateful for all that I have learned from you and the ways in which each of you have touched my life.

A million thanks to the executive directors,

board members, managers, colleagues and associates I have worked with throughout the years. Thank you Alicia S., Bonnie S., Andy S., Ann B., Archie G., Beth H., Billie W., Bob L., Bobby T., Bonda G., Connie R., Ed P., Edee D., Eric P., Forough H., Glenn R., Greg S., Heidi H., Jeff B., Jeff F., Jim S., Jimmy P., Joe B., Joe G., Joe M. (dec'd)., Joe P., John B., John G., Joie A., Justin F., Keith N., Kent S., Kyle S., Larry C., Laura O., Leo D., Mary G., Maryam G., Matt P., Mel S., Mica L., Miguel A., Mike J., Mike L., Mike P., Pam C., Pat S., Peggy F., Poonam K., Randy D., S Patel, Sarah G., Sheila G., Sherry G., Tami B., Vonda S. and Susan R. for your mentoring, advice, words of wisdom and friendship. Many of you were coaches and advisors who provided the guidance I needed to succeed. Others of you reinforced leadership best practices in business and in life as I simply observed how you carried yourself, how you communicated with others and how you made critical decisions. Many of you have become trusted friends. I know the readers of this book will benefit from lessons I learned from you.

To my funeral service industry colleagues, thank you for your inspiration. I learned from each of you and it was a privilege to work side by side with you in the service industry we love. Thank you, Alan Wolfelt, for the profound insights you shared with me and for the single quote that clarified how I want to live my life, "When words are inadequate, have a ceremony." I apply that concept to every aspect of my life. Thank you, Chris K., Christine H., Chuck K., Dick P., Frank S., Jack F. I & II, Johnny P., Julie B., Lauren B., Linda C., Mac C., Mary P., Pam S., Paula Sue R., Ray F., Susan M., Todd vB., Tom M. and especially my Key West study group. The best practice, think-tank meetings I attended twice a year with all of you left me salivating to achieve more. They were energizing. I continually worked hard to take our companies to higher levels of personalized customer care because of you. You are an amazing group of professionals – the best our industry offers. A special thank you to Bill W., Bob L., Dan D., Doug (Peanut) G., Ernie H., Gary F., Gregg S., Jim B., Jim P., John H., Kelly D., Mark K., Matt G., Milton H., Peter M. and Wendy W.

For some of you, I owe an enormous thank you for your patience as I learned valuable lessons through my own mistakes while working with you or for you. Thank you, Amber G., Christina N., Jake S., Michael S. (dec'd), Patrick C. and Tami V. for the difference you made in my life as we dedicated our professional lives to the families we served at Lohman Funeral Homes.

Lastly, I thank Dr. Mary McLeod Bethune. Her legacy of leadership has been a profound influence in my life. Thank you, Nilda Comas, our master sculptor, for the Mary McLeod Bethune marble statue you created for the U.S. Capitol Statuary Hall

State Collection. It has been a tremendous honor to work with you, Sandy S. with the State of Florida and our board of directors Ashley S., Billie W., Bob L., Brent C., Danielle G., Derick H., Jennifer A., Jim C., Joyce C., Kathy C., Mary G., Michelle C., Nellie L. and Sherri L. to honor her as a great Floridian.

When President Bethune reached the age of 78, she wrote her Last Will & Testament as a guiding light for future leaders, continuing to mentor all that would follow, including me some fifty-plus years later. "Truly, my worldly possessions are few. Yet, my experiences have been rich. From them, I have distilled principles and policies in which I believe firmly, for they represent the meaning of my life's work. They are the products of much sweat and sorrow." She recognized as I do that riches are not in the form of worldly possessions, but in the richness of life experiences. She left everyone a beautiful legacy with these inspiring words: "I leave you love, hope, faith, racial dignity, the challenge of developing confidence in one another, the respect for the use of power and the desire to live harmoniously with one another."

About the Author

Nancy Rae Lohman is a businesswoman, philanthropist, community enthusiast and national speaker.

She and her husband, Lowell, their son, Ty, and her brother-in-law, Victor, were formerly the owners of Lohman Funeral Homes, Cemeteries and Cremation, the largest privately owned and operated funeral and cemetery business in Florida. They sold their family business to StoneMor Partners LP in 2012. Recently, Lowell, Ty and Nancy have owned 24 apartment complexes totaling more than 4,000 apartments. Much of her family's business success and philanthropic endeavors are detailed in Lowell's recent book, *The Lohman Way*.

As a licensed funeral director and Certified Funeral & Cemetery Executive (CFCE), Nancy served as president of the ICCFA (International Cemetery, Cremation & Funeral Association), president of the SCCFA (Southern Cemetery, Cremation & Funeral Association) and past board member of the FCCFA (Florida Cemetery, Cremation & Funeral Association). Nancy has been a speaker at conferences and conventions across the United States and Latin America including Ohio, Wisconsin, Washington, Florida, California, Virginia, Arizona, the Dominican Republic and Colombia, South America.

Nancy's career began at Hyatt Hotels, then she was employed by Eastman Kodak Company before joining the family funeral and cemetery business more than 20 years ago. Nancy graduated from The Ohio State University in 1982 with a Bachelor of Science degree, is a lifetime member of the Ohio State Alumni and was the 1981 Ohio State Homecoming Queen. She earned a master's degree in Leadership Communication (MACOML) from Gonzaga University, graduating in May 2017.

Nancy is a leader in many nonprofit organizations. She served as president of the Ormond Memorial Art Museum and Gardens (Ormond Beach, Florida) and is chairing a $3.5 million capital campaign to redesign the building and add museum galleries, classrooms and other amenities. She is a board member of the Halifax Humane Society and chaired a $3.6 million renovation and expansion project that created a pet-centric campus in Daytona Beach, Florida. She serves as a board member and officer for the Council on Aging of Volusia County. She also supports her husband with the Lohman Diabetes Education and Awareness Initiative. She is the chair of the Mary McLeod Bethune Statuary Fund, an organization responsible for bringing to fruition the marble statue of Dr. Mary McLeod Bethune to replace one of Florida's statues in the U.S. Capitol National Statuary Hall Collection in Washington, D.C. She has previously served as president of the

Ormond Beach Chamber of Commerce and president of the Ormond Beach Historical Society.

In addition to other community awards, Nancy was chosen as one of the *Daytona Beach News-Journal*'s top 40 women in business and was awarded the 2018 Most Charitable Award.
She was honored in the past as one of the most influential women in Volusia County. She and her husband received the Mayor's Award for Civic Engagement and received both the Embassy of Hope and the Halifax Humane Society's humanitarian awards. Nancy received the Association of Fundraising Professionals Non-Profit Champion Award and was selected as a recipient of The Ohio State University Distinguished Alumni Award.

She and her husband received the Daytona Regional Chamber of Commerce Lou Fuchs Award, the Council on Aging of Volusia County Glenn & Connie Ritchey Community Service Award, the United Way Community Foundation Herbert M. Davidson Award and the Volusia County Cultural Alliance Tippen Davidson Award.

Nancy and Lowell have donated more than $10 million to the charities and organizations they passionately serve. Most recently was a $4 million gift to Halifax Health Foundation to establish the Lohman Diabetes Center for Excellence and the Lohman Building at Halifax Health in Daytona Beach, Florida.

They have enjoyed extensive traveling, but cherish their home life and the holidays with their treasured pets, Snowball and Miss Peanut.

Contact the Author
Nancy Rae Lohman

Schedule Nancy as a Speaker or
Inquire About her Book.

Website
BlossomForSuccess.com

E-mail
Nancy@BlossomForSuccess.com

Phone
(386) 451-2011

Speaking

Nancy is available to speak to business and civic organizations, nonprofits and other groups. Among the topics and subjects of her motivational and educational speeches are:

- BLOSSOM: Cultivating More Joy and Success in Life and Business
- Leading Yourself to Better Lead Others
- Preparing Yourself to Make a Difference
- Focus on Personal Measures of Success
- Empowering Best Practices

CPSIA information can be obtained
at www.ICGtesting.com
Printed in the USA
FSHW021821010721
82847FS